The Essential Steps Required
to Establish and Maintain
a Successful Firm

THE BUSINESS
OF THE
PRACTICE OF LAW

RODERICK J. McLEOD, Q.C.

For information about this title or to order other books and/or electronic media, contact the publisher:
Roderick J. McLeod
rod.mcleod@telus.net

ISBN: 978-1-7750577-0-3

Printed in the United States of America

Cover and Interior design: 1106 Design

This book is dedicated to that extremely small percentage of the population who are both principled and ethical, who always do the right thing regardless of the monetary or personal cost.

CONTENTS

INTRODUCTION

IF YOU READ MY STORY, you will understand my focus on *the business of the practice of law.*

After graduating from Osgoode Hall Law School in 1971, I was hired by Jack Lamarsh. He was a senior partner in the nine-person firm Mason & Company, located in Calgary, Alberta. I was articled to Blair Mason, who was a well-known and respected civil litigation lawyer. Blair later became a Court of Queen's Bench Justice and subsequently became the Chair of the Alberta Human Rights Commission following his retirement from the Court.

I quickly noticed that Jack Lamarsh was the entrepreneur at Mason & Company. He zeroed in on the business of the practice of law. Blair Mason, on the other hand, looked at the law more as a profession; if you did good work for a reasonable fee, other crass things such as making money would look after themselves.

I also noticed that Jack started his workday early, at least by Mason & Company standards. I began to make a point of getting into the office when he did or just shortly before. Jack and I got into the habit of going for breakfast together at the Standard Life Building cafeteria, located kitty corner to the Pacific 66 Building where Mason & Company had its offices. Having breakfast with him gave me the opportunity to have many conversations with Jack and to learn about the business of the practice of law through his eyes. It was clear that he was a "bottom line" guy and paid really close attention to what the lawyers in the firm billed each month.

Based on my conversations with Jack, I quickly deduced that if I were to have a future with Mason & Company, I'd best start the process of bringing legal work to the firm and paying for myself. Unbeknownst to Jack, I put him in my sights. In terms of billing in the firm, he was the "big kahuna," and the goal I set for myself was to out-bill him.

While that goal took some time to achieve, I went on to out-bill Jack and everyone else at

Mason & Company. In telling you my story, I will explain how I went about becoming the firm's leading biller. Moreover, I'll tell you how I subsequently started my own law firm from scratch.

The lawyers at Mason & Company were pretty laid back. With the exception of Jack Lamarsh and one or two other partners, they seemed comfortable with their respective lots in life and for some reason didn't aspire to make a lot of money practicing law. In fact, they kept saying that one would never get rich doing the work of a lawyer. I firmly believed they were wrong. With the correct approach to the business of the practice of law, you could not only provide first-class legal services to your clients, but you could make some serious money while doing so.

In the early to mid-1970s, when I was getting my start at Mason & Company, Calgary's economy was booming with a capital "B." Real estate prices were rising rapidly in spite of mortgage rates exceeding ten percent and about to go higher. From my earlier days in Calgary, I knew some people in the real estate game, so I went after them to send me legal work. In Alberta, as in other Canadian jurisdictions, a lawyer is required to complete both the purchase and sale of property.

Getting real estate referrals was the fastest way I could think of to increase my billings.

I didn't know otherwise, so when it came to doing the real estate transactions, I emulated Jack Lamarsh. A signed Offer to Purchase would be sent by the real estate company to my attention requesting that I represent either the buyer or the seller of the property in question. (We called buyers and sellers, "vendors" and "purchasers" in those days, but to conform to the plain-language movement, those descriptions were changed to "seller" and "buyer.")

We would then open a file and start dictating letters into our dictation machines. There was a letter to the real estate company acknowledging its letter of instruction and agreeing to accept the retainer. Then, there was a letter to the City of Calgary tax department requesting a tax certificate, with a firm cheque enclosed to pay for the document. We would dictate a letter to the other lawyer advising that we were acting for one of the parties, and so on. Every file, depending on whether you acted for a vendor or a purchaser, was, for all intents and purposes, exactly the same. However, the practice was to dictate every piece of paper or corresponding instruction on the file.

Purely from a volume-of-work perspective, this absolute inefficiency almost killed me. Then, I hired Ms. Sally Lauder as my secretary. When she started her job, I did what I always did and what Jack had taught me to do: I started dictating. It didn't take but a few days for Sally to come into my office for a chat. She asked me what I thought I was doing dictating the same letters over and over again, and instructed me to stop dictating immediately! Sally assured me she knew what to do, and unless there was a problem with a file (and in those days there often were problems), all I had to do was watch the clients sign the papers she had prepared and leave her alone.

Doing things the way Lamarsh did things was "killing me" because his way was so lawyer time intensive. Sally Lauder took on many of the tasks I had been doing, thus freeing my time to increase the volume of work I was able to accomplish. As a result, my billings increased dramatically. In those days, we were jacks of all trades when it came to the law. Thanks to Sally, I now had time to attempt to bring in other work such as wills, estates, incorporations, civil litigation and even criminal matters. It wasn't until later that I decided to specialize in the area of real property and abandon the areas of the law to which others were better suited. When I opened my own firm, I insisted that the firm's lawyers become specialists in one area of the law. It was always a fight, but eventually I prevailed, and the firm prospered beyond my wildest dreams.

As I got busier and busier, I convinced Mason & Company to open a second, smaller office in the south part of Calgary. I found space in a new building on Southport Road and my partners—I was a partner by this time—agreed to my idea. We opened the new south office in the late '70s, and I moved there with about five secretaries and an articling student. We were busy. I had attracted several builder clients, and as a result, we received builder mortgage instructions by the box full.

I promoted the hell out of the place. I would go to real estate offices for their Monday morning meeting, where I would discuss various real estate pitfalls of which the realtors should be wary. Some of the realtors became my friends, and those friendships continue to today. Every lunch hour was another opportunity for promotion. I would take someone for lunch every day.

I worked really hard and soon achieved my goal of out-billing Jack Lamarsh, and by a lot. And not only that, I collected my receivables as well.

The idea of the south office was to be closer to the real estate action and new subdivisions. Any legal work outside the real property area would be referred to the main office to be handled by one of the lawyers there. At least that was the intent. Clients would come to the south office looking for assistance with legal matters not related to real estate, and I would refer them to one of the lawyers in the downtown office. Too often, a few days later, the potential client would call me to advise that he or she had not yet heard from anyone. I would then phone the main office to try to track down the lawyer who had not followed up. Even I had an awful time getting to the lawyer in question. At one point, I phoned the main office to speak to a lawyer—any lawyer—only to be told no one was there. Several of the firm's members had cottages in Windermere, British Columbia, and did not think anything of taking off Thursday night and returning to the office Monday afternoon. This was going on while those of us in the south office were out-of-control busy.

To make my long story short, friends and clients saw what was going on. They started telling me I was crazy to stay with the firm; I should go out on my own.

On September 15, 1980, I opened my own law firm. I was scared to death. I had a wife, a three-year-old son, an infant daughter, a mortgage and a dog. I did not need an alarm clock to get me up in the morning.

The first decision I made turned out to be fortuitous. I decided to locate my office in a market area far removed from the competition of larger law firms. Instead, I concentrated my efforts on serving people and businesses within the geographic market area I had chosen: the suburbs in the southwest and southeast quadrants of our city, Calgary. At the time, there were several hundred thousand people living in these areas. When these folks needed legal services, they were required to venture into the heart of the city, with all the inherent inconveniences of doing so. By opening our office in the growing suburbs, we were able to offer our clients many benefits that traditional law firms could not. Our parking was plentiful and more importantly, free. Our office opened at 7 a.m., we worked until at least 6 p.m., and we had our phones answered by a real person during those hours. In addition, we were able to attract first-class legal secretaries and paralegals who called our area "home." They welcomed the opportunity to live close to their place of employ, especially if they had young children.

Our location and office hours allowed us to meet clients on their way to and from work, and I would accommodate them if they wanted to meet on the weekend.

Obviously, I could not perform all areas of the practice on my own and expect a high level of competency. As my real estate practice flourished, I added lawyers who had expertise in other areas of the law or who had the desire to focus on areas where there was a demand for our services.

Initially, we did a little bit of everything. Looking back, it would be fair to say that in some respects we were not the best suited to do some of the tasks we undertook, and while we worked extra hard to ensure that the quality of our work would at least be acceptable, I was worried about doing legal work at a less than first-class level. As a result, I became convinced that we must become a firm of specialists who practiced law in our geographic market area at a level equal to what the "big boys" did in the city centre. With that goal in mind, I insisted that every member of our firm be a specialist in one of the following areas: wills and estates, real estate and mortgages, civil litigation, corporate commercial or securities. Of course, this process of specialization took years to develop, but when I retired, we had lawyers practicing in all of the areas I just noted.

We did not practice in the areas of tax, administrative or criminal law. We referred clients needing assistance to respected lawyers who specialized in these areas and who treated their clients fairly. We would sometimes help (as long as we did not get in the way), and we were always there to hold our client's hand and translate the legal mumbo jumbo when necessary.

My major secret for success was simple hard work, something I had done all my life. I started work early, and I worked long and late to get a legal task done as quickly as was humanly possible. I never left my office for the day without returning all of my telephone calls. And I was like a bear with a sore ass if the lawyers in my firm did not do the same.

We went through scores of lawyers before finding ones we would hire full-time with McLeod & Company. It did not take me long to get rid of the duds, and believe me, there were many lawyers who just didn't have the work ethic that I demanded. Our front door could, at times, resemble a revolving door. That said, I never asked any member of our firm to do more, or work harder, than I did. I would expect that even my biggest critic at the firm would acknowledge that fact.

During that era, fear was a terrific motivator. I made it clear that I simply would not accept those in our firm who didn't pull their weight. I often reminded members of our firm that we were in the service business. There were lawyers on virtually every corner, and in Canada, law schools were belching out lawyers every year by the thousands. I told them that if we were going to survive, we had to out-service and out-work our competitors.

And you know what? Given my work ethic and the work ethic I instilled in others, the task was not all that difficult. However, too many lawyers are lazy, pure and simple. They aren't prepared to make the sacrifices necessary to be really successful.

When I started my firm, there were just two of us. In the first month of our practice, I billed $50,000 from my real estate practice; my partner billed nothing. My partner had visions of grandeur. He had several secretaries and was losing us money every month. This situation continued for some time, but I simply could not carry the entire firm on my shoulders. After a heart-to-heart conversation, he left, and I fired all his secretaries. I vowed that, if I were to fail, it would be because of me and the decisions I had made, not decisions made by a partner who lacked the will and the ability to succeed. Right then and there, I vowed that this was going to be my firm and I would call the shots.

Eventually I did agree to allow associates in the firm to become partners. Traditionally, lawyers want to be partners, and the people who were my associates were no different. I understood their desire to become part owners of the firm. However, based on my previous experiences with partners, I was reluctant to give up managerial control of the firm. I had worked much too long and hard developing my firm to have folks inject ideas that I did not believe were sound and, in effect, undo what I had been able to accomplish to that point in the firm's growth.

To be fair, the lawyers working at my firm appeared to acknowledge my management abilities, and when they eventually became partners, they not only agreed but for the most part welcomed the insertion of a clause in our Partnership Agreement stipulating that I would be the managing partner or the Chair of the firm's management committee for as long as I remained a partner of the firm. As far as I know, that partnership agreement contractual provision was unique to McLeod & Company.

It is not my intention to be overly self-congratulatory. However, within a comparatively short span of time, our firm became as successful as any firm in Alberta; few, if any, were more successful. I was adamant that I was not about to let any person ruin what I had achieved. I always listened to what my partners had to say and carefully considered their viewpoints on various decisions that needed to be made, but I made the final decision. Fortunately—and I think my former partners will agree—I made more good decisions than I did bad, and the firm's success continued up to the day I retired and, I expect, beyond.

———•———

Throughout this book, you will find my assessment of the lawyers in our firm to be generally negative. I recognize that, and I think my experience of trying to build and run a firm has resulted in this perception.

Not all lawyers in the firm were troublesome. I admit that I was not close to most lawyers from a social perspective or otherwise. It was hard to be a buddy and a boss at the same time. Frankly, the firm was the only thing I had in common with some lawyers. Although I did have friends within the firm, most of the people my wife Brenda and I socialized with were nonlawyers, and I preferred it that way.

Over the following twenty-four years, my firm McLeod & Company grew to twenty-seven lawyers and fifty support staff. The firm occupied 23,000 square feet of space in a building in which I and some of my partners had forty percent ownership. Our partner in the building was Dick Van Grieken, who owned The Telsec Group, a commercial real estate development company operating in the province of Alberta. Dick was, and is, the very best property development guy I have ever met, which is saying something because property development and real estate was what I specialized in as a lawyer. I will tell you more about Dick later.

I ran the joint like a benevolent dictator, and I made no bones about it. However, around 2003, I was getting tired. I had worked like a dog virtually from the time I was a kid.

From as long ago as I can remember, I liked making money...

When I was nine or ten years old, I had my own paper route in Kitchener, Ontario. As well, I would collect six-quart baskets from neighbours, stick them together in a bundle of four baskets, and pile my wagon high with the bundles. Off I would go to the Kitchener Farmer's Market, where I was paid five cents per basket by the Mennonite farmers. In the winter, I can remember shovelling neighbours' sidewalks, without being asked to do so. I would then knock on the neighbours' doors to point out what I had done in the hope they would give me twenty-five cents or something for my unsolicited services.

Around the same time, perhaps when I was a bit older—maybe eleven or twelve years old—the midway arrived during the summer holidays at the Memorial Auditorium site in Kitchener. Our home was very close to the fairgrounds, so I went looking for a job at the midway. For at least two summers, I peeled potatoes and made french fries for a food vendor. I would start work around 10 o'clock in the morning and leave around 11 p.m. The owner of the food booth fed me and paid me seventy-five cents a day.

Looking back over my years at McLeod & Company and my observations of other firms, it became obvious to me that the most successful firms of the day had leaders who could best be described as "hardnosed": Bill Britton at Bennett Jones, Jim Palmer at Burnett Duckworth (although I am told that Jim was a very kind and considerate man as well), and Bill Howard at Howard Mackie. There were others, but the firms that did not have a strong personality at the helm did not do nearly as well; some firms that were run by committee simply did not survive. To me, the demise of certain firms was inevitable. It is too bad they did not have this book to read way back then. If they had had the opportunity to follow my advice, they might still be around today.

So, after a very long introduction, let's get at it.

Why *The Business of the Practice of Law?*

WHILE I WAS IN THE PRO-CESS of building my firm, I could not help but notice that no other lawyer or group of lawyers in my city were doing the same thing. Of course, there were very small firms of one to five people and very large firms that had been established for years. However, no one seemed to be in the process of building a firm like I was.

I vividly remember lawyers from large downtown firms visiting us for various reasons. Their shock that our firm did not reside in a walk-up above a 7-Eleven store was obvious. Our offices were professional, functional and very nice—definitely on a par with the space occupied by our much larger competitors from the downtown core. You could tell they were really surprised when they saw our offices.

I remember one reception at our firm, when the wife of a tax lawyer with a big firm turned to me and commented how pleased I must be with what I had achieved. I thanked her, saying that I hadn't really thought about what had been accomplished, as we were just too busy to stop and appreciate the success we enjoyed.

We were, I believe, unique in building our practice, and I often thought I should write down what we did that seemed to ensure our success. I remember going to a seminar conducted by a lawyer from Mesa, Arizona. The seminar was, ostensibly, designed to teach lawyers the fundamental business aspects of practicing law. This fellow did not tell me anything I did not already know; we had already implemented these concepts in our firm. In fact, I am confident I gave this lad some ideas for him to pass on to others during his future seminars.

That said, I was glad to see such a course being offered. Although it did not help me or my firm, it was, at least, an attempt by the Law Society of Alberta to inject some business acumen into their continuing legal education program. However, I do not recall this course—or any similar courses—ever being offered again.

When I was in law school, the subjects taught were mainly basic courses in torts, contracts, tax, corporate, commercial and business organizations, to name but a few. All of my professors were men who (in my day, the professors were all men) had never practiced law but who had a master's degree or doctorate in the theory of the course they taught. Few had practical hands-on experience.

There were, however, a few professors who had worked in law firms. Their ability to bring home a legal point, backed up by real-life experience, was refreshing. They made it so much easier for the students to grasp and understand the subject at hand. These guys were few and far between; generally speaking, they taught part-time and came from the ranks of big, established law firms. However, these lawyers were not required to generate business in their firm, as their firm's business was— and had been for some considerable time—well-secured by those who had gone before. As such, they were not able, nor were they qualified, to instruct us about the business of the practice of law.

My law school experience...

After graduating from Simon Fraser University in Vancouver, BC, I applied to four schools: Osgoode Hall Law School in Toronto, the University of Toronto Faculty of Law, the University of British Columbia Law School, and the University of Alberta Law School. The University of Toronto Faculty of Law relied almost exclusively on grades to assess incoming students, and they took one hundred and fifty students with the highest grades. While I knew my chances of getting into that place were slim, I thought I had a fighting chance at the others.

To shorten the story, I was not accepted at the University of Toronto, but I was accepted at the University of British Columbia and Osgoode Hall. In keeping with their past practices of not accepting me, I was denied admittance at the University of Alberta. Given that the more prestigious schools had accepted me, I thought their refusal of my application a rather laughable position for the university to take. So, the result is I have two university degrees in spite of the Alberta educational system. I have noticed, however, that the province of Alberta readily accepted the king's ransom in taxes I have paid them during my working years.

I decided to accept Osgoode's offer because I was not a fan of the Vancouver culture or work ethic.

One thing about Simon Fraser I did not like was the fact it was full of left-leaning hippies. There were a lot of really weird-looking and -acting people who vocally supported positions they agreed with but shouted down anyone with an opposing viewpoint. We had bomb scares in the library just before exams, and we had myriad protests for one fool reason or another. Having to endure these people was not a pleasant experience at the time. So, when I decided on a law school, I wanted the oldest, most conservative place I could find, and my choices were Osgoode or Dalhousie. Osgoode was closer, located in Toronto, and, as a bonus, my aunt and uncle lived there and offered to have me stay at their home while attending law school.

I arrived in Toronto in late August of 1968. After visiting various relatives in the Ottawa Valley (I was born in Renfrew), I started law school. On a somewhat funny note, I was given a lot of materials when I registered, but one document in particular caught my attention. It was the class schedule. Now, everyone thought that law school was a real grind, and they entered that arena with some fear and trepidation. I looked at the schedule of classes and was shocked. I knew law school was going to be tough, but what

I was looking at seemed ridiculous. Some days there were eight hours of classes, and the shortest day had five hours. What had I gotten myself into? Then it dawned on me: the schedule I thought was for first-year students was, in fact, a schedule for all three years, and our actual schedule was fifteen hours a week.

Much more civilized.

Both types of professors—the lawyer/professors and the career professors—did not know the important aspects of the business of the practice of law. The professors had never experienced the need to generate business and cover overhead. The part-time lawyer/professors didn't know much about generating business because legal work was readily available to them within their firm, and they had office managers at their beck and call who catered to their every need.

Accordingly, the business aspect of a law practice was never offered as a course at law school, primarily because no one knew what it was all about. Too many theorists snubbed their noses at the crass aspect of making money when a gentleman's professionalism was preferable. There seemed to be this belief that, when you became a lawyer, it was more important to be what was considered a "professional" and not stoop so low as to want to turn a law firm into a successful and profitable enterprise.

Of course, the big firms made money and lots of it. However, the legal work came from long-established relationships that, of course, were not enjoyed by someone starting his or her own firm. Individuals going out on their own had absolutely no practical training in the day-to-day functioning of a law firm. They learned by the seat of their pants and either succeeded or failed. In fact, there are many stories of lawyers who, were it not for their spouses' employment, would have starved to death. They had absolutely no idea how to go about establishing a successful law firm.

It is my hope that any young lawyer who does not fit the big-firm mold may, by reading my book, get some ideas that will help that person succeed in a very difficult and competitive business. Even if these young people choose the life of a big-firm lawyer and do not aspire to opening their own firms, they can still learn a lesson or two about how to rise within the ranks of the biggest of law firms. Briefly, the old adage that "the guy with the gold makes the rules" applies even to a big-firm environment. If you want to work in a big firm and you want to prosper, get busy and make your firm money. Believe me: billing a lot of money or getting a lot of work in the firm's door (both of which translate to making money, and thus the gold), will enhance your reputation amongst senior-partner decision-makers. As a result, you will rise in the ranks within a partnership substantially faster than your colleagues.

1

THE GOLDEN RULES

THE REAL GOLDEN RULE— "Do unto others as you would have them do unto you"—perfectly and succinctly gives us a basic guide for successful interpersonal relationships.

While many other things go into ensuring that relationships are successful, these basic eleven words, if adhered to, set the stage for getting along with our fellow humans. I try my best to live by these very wise words even though I do not consider myself a religious person.

Obviously the Golden Rules I adapted for *The Business of the Practice of Law* is a takeoff on the biblical version, but if the four simple yet simplistic rules I state below are followed, a lawyer starting his or her own practice should be successful.

1. Get the legal work in the door.

2. Do the legal work quickly, efficiently and well.

3. Promptly send out a reasonable bill.

4. Make sure to collect what is owed you.

While this formula for success is quite straightforward and simple, for too many young lawyers it's not straightforward and simple at all. They have absolutely no idea how to go about getting legal work in the door. They have never been taught how to go about attracting clients, and as a result, they are content to do whatever work a more senior lawyer passes on to them.

In fact, the big firms do not need the work, and most large firms do not encourage their young lawyers to even try to attract new clients. Here's why: some senior partners have, over the years, developed relationships that translated into ongoing legal work—and lots of it. The current senior partners probably inherited the firm's clients from a prior generation of entrepreneurial lawyers and were able to do a good job servicing these clients over the years. As their clients' businesses grew and flourished, the firm grew larger as well, and the legal business became self-perpetuating.

It is extremely difficult and very expensive for established businesses to change lawyers. As long as the current senior partners are successful in maintaining the various relationships with clients and the existing lawyers don't do anything really stupid, chances are that a client will continue with its current law firm for many years. Big clients beget big law firms. And the boys and girls (primarily boys) who have worked their way up the firm's bureaucracy to senior partner status maintain the relationships with existing clients and make really big bucks in the process.

However, young lawyers with an entrepreneurial bent do not aspire to that kind of work life or that kind of life, at least not for the long term. They aspire to something different. After a reasonable period of time learning the ins and outs of the practice of law, the lawyer with an entrepreneurial bent looks for a better and more prosperous lifestyle—not an easier lifestyle but a more rewarding and less political one.

That is the person I had in mind when I decided to write this book. The entrepreneurial lawyer would, pretty quickly, figure out how to be successful at the practice of law, but the purpose of this book is to make the journey just a little bit easier.

One can assume, sometimes unreasonably, that those who graduate from law school know or have a general understanding of the subject. However, most people are not blessed with a natural business sense. The vast majority go to work, do the job they are hired to do, go home to their families to participate in family activities, or just watch television or play games on their computers. They get up the next morning and do the same thing all over again.

While these folks are doing their job, the business owner is concentrating on making the business a success. This person eats, sleeps, breathes and dreams about the business twenty-four hours a day. This person is an entrepreneur. It is my theory that entrepreneurs are born, not made. The absolute best business people I have met never stepped foot inside a university. The ranks of middle management are filled with those with MBA degrees who attended business schools and think they are entrepreneurs. They either end up in government or in a middle-management job in a well-established corporation. It is the exception for someone to go to business school and then become an entrepreneur. As noted, in my experience, entrepreneurs are born with the inherent ability to start a successful business, employ a large number of people who pay taxes, and make a lot of money in the process. Success is not hard for them; it is just second nature.

The practice of law is similar. A person graduating from law school could be the gold medal winner, know legal theory inside and out, but if that person does not understand "The Golden Rules" of the practice, he or she will never master the business of the practice of law.

My introduction to Economics...

I was not a great student. I found school boring; the teachers at Central High School in Calgary seemed old and disinterested. While I enjoyed sports, I didn't enjoy physics, chemistry, and the like. While I was in high school, I was working between sixteen and twenty hours a week. By Sunday I was tired. I didn't have time for a very active social life, and studying for Monday's classes on Sunday just didn't seem like a priority.

At that time in Alberta, in order to get admitted to university, you needed an appropriate average grade in Mathematics, Physics or Biology, Chemistry, Social Studies, English, and French. I had real trouble with Mathematics and French. At the end of my last year of high school, I didn't have a passing grade in either subject. I decided to go back for a fourth year of high school and repeat grade twelve, but at Henry Wisewood, a relatively new high school closer to my home. I knew many of the students at that school, so attending a new school was not the least bit traumatic for me, and I enjoyed my time at Wisewood.

I decided that if I was going to go back to grade twelve for a year (they did not have semester systems at that time), I might as well make the time worthwhile and try and get my average up. So, I took Math, French, Biology, Chemistry and an elective described as "Economics." I had a wonderful Chemistry teacher by the name of Gordy Millar, who, unlike the old goat who taught the subject at Central, made the experience interesting and even enjoyable.

The other courses I took were, with one exception, an extension of the boredom I had previously endured. That one exception was Economics. I didn't even know what economics was. However, I read the course outline, and it sounded like something that would interest me. The Economics teacher was Les Nuttall, who turned out to be the absolute best teacher I have ever had. It seemed to me that, for just about all of my schooling, it was as if I had been sitting in a dark room, and then, suddenly, a fellow by the name of Les Nuttall switched on the light. Finally, finally, I was learning things that really mattered to me. I learned about micro and macroeconomics: how government policies affected our economy and how small businesses worked. I was taught about supply and demand and various tried-and-true economic laws. For the first time since leaving Kitchener, I just loved going to class. The education system in Kitchener was superior to what I found in Calgary. That said, had I stayed in Kitchener, I doubt that I would have gone on to university, as many of my Kitchener pals finished high school and went to work.

Before enrolling in Les Nuttall's Economics class, I had absolutely no idea what I would take if I went to university. My mother was constantly at me to get "just one degree," but in what? Now I knew. But the problem I now faced was getting into university. I had failed French again, and the powers that be at the University of Alberta and the newly opened University of Calgary would not let me enroll in their schools without French 30. So, off to Mount Royal College I went to take a semester of French and

Math 30 in the hopes of passing French and raising my grade in Math.

While I was at Mount Royal, my dad had been in Vancouver opening a new Loblaw store. He brought me back an article from one of the Vancouver newspapers concerning a new University to be built on Burnaby Mountain and to be called Simon Fraser University. And from what I could determine, SFU didn't give a hoot if I had French 30 or not. I absolutely hated taking French, and this news was such a relief and so welcome to me that words cannot describe my feelings.

As my educational experience had taken longer than most, I was in a hurry to get through university. I came home the first summer and worked for the City of Calgary Parks Department. Everyone thought that being a parks employee was an easy job, but they had not met our boss. I cannot remember his name, but he was a Hungarian refugee who had immigrated to Canada after the 1956 revolution against Russian communist rule. I don't know if this lad just enjoyed working hard or was worried he would lose his job if he didn't work full out. Suffice it to say that he kept me busy, and I would come home at day's end hot, dirty and tired. But I made money to go back to school.

I started my second year of university in September of 1966, and as Simon Fraser was on a semester system, I just kept going to school until I was finished. After five semesters without a break, I graduated with a bachelor's degree in Economics and three credits short of a bachelor's degree in both Economics and Commerce.

Simon Fraser was a unique university. During my time there, I took more than twenty economics and commerce courses, and I enjoyed every one. There were six full professors in the Economics and Commerce faculty, not bad for a university with a total student body of fewer than three thousand students. We were taught by economists who had been advisors to presidents of the United States and others; for example, WM Scammel was an instructor and a world-recognized expert on International Monetary Policy.

I was being taught by Dr. Scammel when the price of gold was allowed to float. I couldn't help but think, "If I only had money." I knew from my professor's teachings that the price of gold was going in one direction. I tried to get my dad to buy gold, but that idea was hard for him to understand. After I graduated from law school, I got my dad into various real estate deals that made him money and assisted him in his retirement years.

RULE #1

Get the Legal Work in the Door

▶ The first Golden Rule, Get the Legal Work in the Door, is much easier said than done. To point out the obvious, you may be the best lawyer in the history of the Western world, but if you do not have the work to enable you to show off your talents, you will be like the proverbial "tree falling in the forest that makes no sound" because there will be no one present to witness your legal abilities.

The second and more practical reason to comply with this Rule is to avoid starving to death! Without work to do, you cannot make money, perpetuate your practice, contribute to your and your family's well-being, and—on an even more basic level—survive.

I may be repeating myself, but the absolute most important aspect of the practice of law is getting the legal work in the door. If you cannot master that Rule, you are dead in the water, and you should reconsider ever opening your own firm as you will be doomed to failure.

From a practical point of view, I believe this Rule is the most important of the bunch. It is a demanding Rule that must be on your mind every working hour and in your dreams as well. You must always be on the lookout for business—and not just the "dog bite" cases. You must ingratiate yourself with people who can send you work on an ongoing basis. Do not kid yourself; this is really hard work, and very few lawyers are any good at the task.

When I retired and was invited to cocktail parties, I was finally able to relax at such an event and not have an overpowering urge to work the room in the never-ending hunt for new business.

I will try to give you the help you need to satisfy Rule 1 and the other Rules that follow.

2

CLIENT RELATIONSHIPS

DEVELOPING CLOSE, enduring client relationships is fundamentally important if a firm is to be successful. And these relationships take time to develop. As I have pointed out, the hardest part of the practice of law—or any service-related business, for that matter—is getting the work in the door. You get the best repeat business as the result of relationships you develop. Developing these long-term successful relationships is a full-time job that requires a dogged determination and a thick skin to deal with rejections.

The best way to develop relationships is to follow the first three of my Golden Rules. Nothing works better to develop and maintain relationships than doing really good work, doing it on time and charging a fee that is commensurate with the value of the job. As well, if you are trying to impress a client, it is not necessary to charge them for every meeting or phone call. Use your head. You might be wise to, as they say, lose money on the apples and make it up on the oranges. If a client has a son or daughter buying a house or needing a Will, consider doing the work for just disbursements. Nothing will cement a relationship faster than doing a favour for a client's child.

Relationship building was, for me, common sense. Too many lawyers are fixated on their billings and short-term status within the firm to accept the fact that a rigid approach to the solicitor/client relationship, as far as billings are concerned, is incredibly short-sighted and works against developing relationships so critical to getting work in the door, and thus, the long-term success of a firm.

▶ *Build successful relationships that lead to business.*

I tried my best to teach the young lawyers in my firm how to get business in the door. I encouraged them to use our firm's resources to help them be successful in that regard. Each lawyer had an expense account, access to Calgary Flames hockey tickets, promotional items such as golf balls, shirts, pens, writing pads, coffee mugs, along with unique Christmas gifts, client lunches and cocktail parties. They had access to virtually everything and anything that they might need to be successful in attracting business to the firm.

As most lawyers had no idea where to start, I would try to help them. I would ask a young lawyer to provide me with a list of ten potential clients. They could be friends, relatives, class-mates or friends of family. Virtually anyone who would potentially need the services of a lawyer could be put on their list. Once I received the list, I would ask the lawyer to reduce the names down to the best five prospects. I would then suggest that the young lawyer use all of the resources available to all our lawyers to court the five people on the list. Inviting a prospective client to lunch was a good start.

I never, ever, had someone refuse an invitation to lunch. Lawyers have an ace in the hole when it comes to the public. Nonlawyers, rightly or wrongly, attach a certain mystique to those of us who have gone to law school and passed the bar admission exams. To have lunch with a lawyer is, in the minds of most laymen, something to look forward to. After all, one does not take a client for lunch at Arby's; the venue is usually a really nice restaurant.

I suggest that the five potential clients be courted in a reasonable manner. Getting to know the invitee slowly over a period of months is better than being in a hurry. Eventually you will find out about the person's likes and dislikes, their political persuasion, their family, their interests and their dreams. If you're lucky, you will make a new friend, and now promoting that new friend will no longer be a chore; you will find it enjoyable. At some point in the relationship, you will know inherently when to ask for the new friend's legal work; you'll ask for a chance to show what you can do to benefit your friend's business.

Now, this idea does not work all the time. Invariably, one or more of the five potential clients will turn out to be someone to whom you simply do not relate. Dump that potential client quickly. Go back to your original list of ten people, replace the dud with a new name, and start again. Do not spend a lot of time with someone who, in your gut, you know is a waste of your time and the firm's money. Move on.

> *My Advice:* *Use the resources of your firm to court five potential clients in a reasonable manner; lunches are a good start. Ideally, you are looking to develop a long-term relationship. Do not be impatient. Take your time. A successful law firm is based on relationships. Do not ever forget that.*

Making it easy to entertain clients...

We had a client who owned an Italian restaurant. The restaurant was very good, with the added benefit of being close to our office. I arranged with the owner for our firm to have a charge account with his restaurant. He liked this arrangement because he did not have to pay a credit card fee. I liked it because when lawyers took clients for lunch at this restaurant, all they had to do was sign the bill at the end of the meal with a note of who they were entertaining, add the appropriate tip, and then off they would go.

Each month the restaurant owner sent me an invoice with the bills attached showing who was entertained and who did the entertaining. Having this documentation was important for two reasons: I wanted to see who was being entertained and who was doing the entertaining, and we had a record of our expenditures should Revenue Canada ask us to justify our client-promotion expenses.

▶ *Building and maintaining client relationships is not the job of the marketing department.*

I believe that the senior partners of any size firm simply cannot abdicate the responsibility of client maintenance and the promotion of new clients to nonlawyers in a marketing department. If you agree with me that relationships are key to attracting meaningful, repeat legal work, the steps leading up to the establishment of these relationships should not, I repeat, should *not,* be left up to a young person in a marketing department. The task is just too important. If you do that, you leave the door open for a competitor to steal your client. Just ask the lawyers who were once employed by larger, prominent law firms that no longer exist.

I believe there is a place for a firm's employees to pay for themselves as a firm grows by doing things like making sure clients are remembered on special occasions and other tasks that assist lawyers in keeping in touch with their clients. However, the primary marketing tasks must always be the responsibility of the lawyers in the firm who have an entrepreneurial bent. They will instinctively know how to market the firm's services and do a much more credible job than any marketing department.

> *My Advice: Don't assign promotion of new clients, and the maintenance of relationships with existing clients, to nonlawyers in a so-called "marketing department." Instead, make it the job of the entrepreneurial lawyers in the firm who know how to market the firm's services.*

Holidays were workdays for me as a kid...

When my family first moved to Calgary, obviously, I had no friends. Sitting in the Bluebird Motel during the grey Calgary days in February, I was bored to death and really missed my friends in Kitchener. I had not as yet started school in Calgary.

To show my mother some pity and to get this sulking fourteen-year-old out of her presence, my dad took me to work with him. My father gave me an apron and put me under the care and control of a produce manager at one of the new Loblaw stores.

Five years later, and I was still working Thursday nights, Friday nights, all day Saturday, Easter holidays, Christmas and summer holidays. I literally had to beg to get a Friday night off when I played senior football for Central High School. During my five years at Loblaw working part-time, I think I ended up working at all the Calgary stores at one time or another and became reasonably proficient looking after a produce stand. I worked really hard. I didn't walk from point A to point B—I jogged. If I didn't out-work everyone, I heard about it from my dad.

▸ *Do special things for your clients on special days of the year.*

I spent a great deal of time and money deciding on a Christmas gift that would capture the attention of our clients and, in many cases, their families. A client's spouse liking the gift we sent to the family was an invaluable bonus.

I picked a variety of gifts, everything from snuggle blankets with our name discreetly placed in small print at one corner of the blanket to gift baskets that were put together by my wife Brenda, and which were by far the absolute nicest baskets anyone had ever seen. The baskets contained fine wine—red and white—wine glasses, Bernard

Callebaut chocolates, gourmet coffee, special jelly beans, mixed nuts of the highest quality, and much, much more. The baskets were beautifully wrapped and weighed about twenty-five pounds. These gifts were given to our better clients, and they loved them, especially when they heard that my wife had shopped for and prepared the baskets all on her own time.

Today, many firms no longer buy their clients gifts at Christmas time. Instead, they send their clients a card advising that in lieu of gifts they made a cash donation to one or more charities. They never say how much they donated. Seldom do they specify the charities that were the recipients. This substitute form of client acknowledgement is a wonderful opportunity missed and is the lazy person's idea of promotion. When I receive such a card, I am always tempted to write and ask for my share of the tax receipt. Of course, I have never done that, but a firm that takes such an approach is depreciated in my eyes. They could have done so much more to ingratiate themselves with their clients. Not very smart and, as noted above, a golden opportunity squandered. By the way, that is what my old firm has resorted to doing. This must be a new form of marketing suggested by the firm's marketing department.

> *My Advice:* *Be sure to do special things for your clients on special days of the year. Birthdays, anniversaries, Christmas… and whatever you do, do not forget Thanksgiving. It is a perfect day to remember your clients and give thanks for allowing you to do their legal work. The vast majority of law firms, big and small, do not take advantage of the opportunity presented by Thanksgiving, so when you do, the impact is great. Your clients will be impressed.*

The support of my wife, Brenda, was essential to my success...

As a twenty-five-year-old, straight male working for the summer in Ottawa, I had my eyes peeled for potential female company. I noticed that there were several good-looking young ladies working at the Department of Consumer and Corporate Affairs, Combines Investigation Branch. One in particular caught my eye. She had a spring in her step, a bubbly personality, and was very attractive. After a brief period of time, I got up the nerve to ask her for lunch. She accepted, and we started dating.

I returned to Ottawa to work for the same department the following summer, and Brenda Zappa and I continued to see one another. I was scheduled to graduate with a law degree that spring and had accepted an articling job with Mason & Company in Calgary for the spring of 1971. I knew maintaining a long-distance relationship would be difficult so before I headed west to commence my articles, I asked her to marry me. Brenda accepted, and we were married in Ottawa on July 30, 1971.

When I was thinking about opening my own firm, I knew being successful in that venture would be far from easy. I also realized that such a step would be time intensive and that I would have to work harder than I had ever worked before. Finally and possibly most importantly, I knew I needed Brenda's unqualified support. It would be so much more difficult for me to be successful if I did not have my family's unconditional backing. So, before I made the decision to go out on my own, I had a chat with Brenda and explained that this idea I was considering was going to be the hardest thing I had ever done, and I asked for her support. I told her that I might be late for dinners she had prepared or that I might miss certain family gatherings because of demands at my new firm. I undertook to be considerate and keep her informed if I was going to be late, and I promised never to take her for granted.

Brenda encouraged me to go ahead and open the firm, and she agreed to do everything she could do to help me make sure the new firm was a success. She did not let me down—not once. She was understanding when work-related matters made me late for one thing or another, just like she said she would be.

After starting my new firm, I employed many of the business promotion ideas suggested in this book, and Brenda always rolled up her sleeves and did what she could to help. Whether it was choosing Christmas gifts for clients, discussing bonuses for staff, buying art work for our office, picking office furniture, making all the food for client receptions at our office or hosting firm parties at our home, Brenda was always there with a big smile on her face to either do all the work or help see that the tasks were completed properly and well. Brenda lived up to her agreement to do what she could to ensure the success of the firm. She became my very best partner in more ways than one.

While Brenda was helping me with the firm, she also had a full time job as Matthew and Hillary's mother, a task she performed extraordinarily well. Today, as our children are mature adults, I know they recognize and appreciate what an outstanding mother they were blessed with having. In fact, Hillary tells me that her mother is her best friend, and Matthew has inherited Brenda's kindness and love of family and family traditions.

I have absolutely no doubt that I could not have accomplished what I did without Brenda's help, support and understanding. She made a most difficult journey easier. The lesson is: get your family's support if you decide to start your own firm. Without total family commitment, you may still be successful, but the task will be considerably more difficult to achieve.

► *Hold regular luncheons for your clients, in your offices.*

I had an idea that firm luncheons would be good for generating business. We had a really nice boardroom on the eighth floor of the South Centre Executive Tower and an even bigger and nicer one when we moved into our Bannister Road offices. My thought was to use these facilities to try to attract business while at the same time give attendees the opportunity to network with people they might be able to do business with.

The luncheons were catered by various restaurants in the area.

Now, when I decided to have these luncheons, I was serious about it, so serious that we would hold luncheons every day for a month, take a break, and then do it again. It was not easy, but these luncheons were really well received. At a typical luncheon, we would, for example, invite a builder, a banker, a major sub trade, a politician, an insurance company representative and someone from the financial securities industry. Or we would invite the entire office of a small brokerage firm. We would make sure that the lawyers specializing in an area of interest to the attendees would be present and say a few words on one topic or another. I would usually wrap up by giving a brief history of our firm and reminding everyone that we would be honoured to do their legal work should the opportunity present itself. We had brochures printed that told the story of our firm and described our areas of specialization.

These luncheons were hard work and could become tedious at times, but they worked. We enhanced existing relationships and developed new ones. I think the people who attended looked forward to being invited back.

My Advice: Firm luncheons give your firm the opportunity to network with potential clients and for your clients to network with one another. The luncheons are hard work but worth it.

▸ **Receptions and dinners are a chance to meet potential clients. Be sure to work the room!**

I was often invited to receptions of one sort or another. I treated those invitations as an opportunity to meet potential clients and, as they say, "work the room."

I remember attending a black tie dinner at Calgary's Westin Hotel and being seated at a table with the head of the Calgary Health Region. Now, believe it or not, the Calgary Health Region had lots of legal work, and some of that work centred on the construction of new and very large structures. It just so happened that I had met the head of the Calgary Health Region when he was a Deputy Minister in the Provincial Government. We had always gotten along very well and had some mutual friends. Well, after a couple of glasses of wine and some friendly banter back and forth, I just decided to ask him how we would go about getting some legal work from the Health Region. His reply was typical of this lad: "Well, the first thing you do is ask." I thanked him and told him I would be in touch. It was not long before we were given big jobs to do on behalf of the Health Region, and we did the work really well and for a fair price. Remember, when the time is right (and you will sense when it is), don't be afraid to "ask" for the work.

> ***My Advice:*** *I have no real words of wisdom in this regard except that it is important to accept invitations to various functions, for no other reason than to "show your firm's flag." The idea is for you to try to pinpoint attendees at the reception who could send business to your firm, and then try to ingratiate yourself with that person or persons.*

▸ **Breakfast clubs, service clubs and political-party meetings are great places to meet potential clients and build relationships.**

Breakfast clubs, service clubs and political parties can present great opportunities for meeting possible future clients and people who have the potential to send you business. Good business, because these folks are, generally speaking, business people who need legal advice from time to time. These groups are perfectly suited to start developing the relationships that in the long term will show dividends for your firm and for you personally as the originating lawyer.

Remember: developing client relationships is crucial to the success of your firm. It can take a lot of time, but it's a terrific feeling when a person you've met through one of these organizations calls you and wants you to do some legal work for them. That success gives you the impetus to go at developing business for your firm with even more intensity. You have tasted the success that comes from proper marketing, and if you are a true entrepreneur, it's a wonderful feeling—an adrenalin rush.

> *My Advice: Joining service clubs, breakfast clubs and political parties is a great way to raise your profile and get work. Encourage your firm's lawyers to get involved with their communities and join these clubs to build relationships with potential clients.*

▸ *Get involved in your community.*
Over and above attending meetings and functions at breakfast clubs and the like, volunteering for service clubs, political parties and charitable

groups is a great way to develop potential business, with the added benefit of making a contribution to your community.

Now, some lawyers I know turned volunteering into an art form. They joined anything and everything, totally neglecting their practice and their partners. They got addicted to the limelight and in the process abused their obligations to their firm. This is not what I mean when I suggest that you get involved in your community. Try to find something that interests you. It makes it so much easier to volunteer if the cause in question captures your imagination.

As a youngster, I was very involved in my community...

I loved Kitchener. It was a wonderful place to grow up. I was involved with Cub Scouts. When we went on paper drives to raise money, there on the truck was the owner of Dare Foods helping us with the fundraising venture. His two boys, Brian and Graham, were members of the same troop. Schneider's Foods, Greb Shoes, Arrow Shirts, Smiles & Chuckles chocolate factory and, of course, Dare Foods and others had their beginnings in this most industrious of cities.

I played Mighty Mite football and minor hockey in a league that was run by the City of Kitchener Police Service. A pretty good idea in that my pals and I grew up holding peace officers in the highest regard. They were all excellent role models for young boys.

I was the Chair (back then we called it "Chairman") of the citizens' board of directors for Canada's first Crime Stoppers Program. In conjunction with the City of Calgary Police Service and local media, the citizens' board was responsible for raising money and running the program.

I think most people are aware of Crime Stoppers or Silent Witness programs; they are just one crime-fighting tool to assist police departments in apprehending people who have committed crimes. The idea is that informants are paid a reward for information provided to the Crime Stoppers Program that resulted in an arrest (not the arrest and conviction but simply the arrest) of someone who had allegedly broken the law. The key is that the informant's identity remained confidential.

This idea caught my imagination, and my colleagues on the citizens' board worked really hard to make the Calgary Crime Stoppers Program a success. Eventually our efforts were adopted by municipalities across Canada.

Not only did I gain great satisfaction from being a member of the citizens' board, I gained several clients and equally as important, long-lasting friendships.

Getting involved in politics opens the door to a wide variety of potential clients. I became a director of a constituency association in my area, and I did so primarily to find out what it was they did. I volunteered my time to knock on doors with the candidate, pass out political propaganda leaflets and, of course, help the association raise money.

I stayed involved for a few years, but I found I did not like the tasks I was expected to perform. It was my experience that the majority of those involved in politics had made that involvement their life's work, literally. That volunteer job consumed their lives. The folks I met were really good people and were the backbone of a successful political party. While I had wanted to give it a try, I found it just wasn't for me. However, in the process, I gained several new clients, one of whom was a major automobile dealership.

Of course, I did other things. I organized golf tournaments, coached minor sports teams, and sat on the boards of the private schools my children attended. All of these activities raised my profile in the community and resulted in legal work for my law firm.

I stress the importance of having a passion for whatever role you take on in the world of giving back to your community. If you get involved, do the very best job you possibly can. Don't do what too many people do: get involved for the sole purpose of enhancing one's resume. If you do that, you will defeat the purpose and be perceived by all as being a phoney, and rightly so.

My Advice: Volunteer in your community. Not only will you gain a lot of satisfaction while contributing to your community; you may gain clients and long-lasting friendships as well.

As an adult, I continued to be very involved in my community...

I coached hockey for nine years, helped organize the Calgary Crime Stoppers Association, and became the first chair of its Board of Directors. I was on the Board of Directors of the William Roper Hull Home for wayward children and for five years organized and chaired the Willow Park Charity Golf Classic. This tournament established the template for charitable golf tournaments in Calgary, and since its inception has raised in excess of ten million dollars. I have been on the Board of Directors of both private and public corporations, conducted seminars in real property law, was the Chair of the Real Property Section of the Canadian Bar Association, Southern Alberta Branch, and for a short time I was a member of the Board of Directors of a political constituency association. And finally, when I retired, I was appointed to the Alberta Securities Commission (ASC), an appointment I really enjoyed. As a bonus, I got to meet David Linder, who is and has been for some time the Executive Director of that organization. I also met Steve Sibold, who was, for part of my appointment, the Chair of the ASC. Not only are both men terrific lawyers, but more importantly to me, they are first-class individuals who I am really proud to call my friends.

I point out the above not for accolades that, frankly, during my career were seldom if ever forthcoming; rather, I want to emphasize that having an economically sound practice does not necessarily mean you cannot contribute to your community at the same time. You need a bit more energy than the average person, but helping others is a way to enrich your life while complementing your efforts to be successful at the business of the practice of law.

▶ *Banks: be careful. They are not your friends.*

The banks made money on our trust account deposits. With the exception of a small percentage that the bank was obligated to pay to the Alberta Law Foundation, our deposits were free money to the banks, as we were not allowed to earn interest on our trust accounts. You can understand why all banks had law-firm trust accounts in their sights. In return for depositing trust funds, a bank would promise to reciprocate by sending the law firm bank-generated business which, of course, the bank's client paid for.

Anyway, this one particular bank courted us with promises of work if we would deposit trust funds with them. We decided to move some trust fund deposits to this bank, and we sat back to wait for the legal work to arrive. It did not. I paid some attention to their reneging on our deal, but we were so busy I didn't dwell on the fact that the bank was not living up to their end of the bargain.

Enter my pal, partner and good friend, Allan Kolinsky. Al and I met on our very first day as articling students when our principals were conducting an Examination for Discovery and we tagged along. Al and I became friends and frequently had lunch together. Years passed, and

after much coaxing, Al finally accepted my offer
to join McLeod & Company. Al's areas of expertise were real estate, mortgages, banking law and
foreclosures. With the exception of foreclosures,
our practices were similar, and our offices were
close to one another. We continued our frequent
lunches; in fact, our get-togethers continue to this
day. Al is a good and decent man who donates a
considerable amount of time to numerous charitable causes. Al has been and continues to be a
really good friend whom I look forward to spending time with and enjoying a laugh or two.

Back to the story: although I was not paying
close attention to what the bank was *not* doing, Al
was. I had raised with the bank manager the lack
of work coming from his branch. His response was
to say, it was a funny thing but the bank just didn't
have any work to send to lawyers. Al kept pointing
out to me that this was not true and backed it up
by showing me the *Business Prospects* magazine,
a publication which, among other things, listed
who had commenced legal actions and against
which defendants. Finally, one day, Al came into
my office with the aforesaid publication in hand
and showed me that this bank had, once again,
sent work to a particular lawyer whom Al had

noticed was getting a lot of work. The lawyer's daddy was a big client of the bank and was no doubt putting heat on the bank manager to help out his son.

Enough was enough! While Al was in my office, I called our accounting department and instructed them to move all our trust accounts to another bank. It was a great deal of money. Within two days, several partners of the firm came into my office to advise that they had received calls from the bank manager concerning the removal of all our trust accounts. They did not know anything about the matter and told the banker as much.

It appeared that he was hesitant to make the most obvious call: the call to me. Finally he did call to ask why we had moved our trust accounts. My reply was that it was the funniest damn thing: one morning, a few days ago, I had arrived at work, and my phone started ringing. Everyone on whose behalf we had deposited funds with his bank instructed me to move their accounts to another lender. We were merely following our clients' instructions. "Now," I said, "if you believe that, I will believe that your bank had no work to send our firm. So now, let's start from scratch. If you send us business, we will consider re-opening trust accounts with your bank."

We ended up having a much better and more profitable arrangement with the bank to which I had moved the trust accounts.

My Advice: Pay attention to how much benefit you are receiving from reciprocal agreements. If you are holding up your end of the deal, but the other side is not, take action.

3

PROMOTING YOUR LAW FIRM

IN MY EXPERIENCE, while many lawyers think they are good at promoting business, few are. The fact of the matter is that, in most successful firms, a small minority of lawyers keep the remaining majority busy.

I remember talking to a friend of mine who was, at the time, the managing partner in a firm of more than eighty lawyers. I asked him how many of the lawyers in the firm generated business. His reply was "four or five." So, six percent of the lawyers in his firm were able to generate enough work to keep the other ninety-four percent busy. The six percent were the entrepreneurs in the firm, and I expect they took home much more money than the ninety-four percent doing the work and who could easily be replaced. Replacing the entrepreneurial lawyer is considerably more difficult.

In general, do everything you can to keep your firm's name in front of your clients. If you start neglecting your clients, someone just like me will be lurking in the wings ready and anxious to step up and steal your clients. Always operate as if you are scared to death that someone else will promote your client away because you became too complacent.

▷ *Assign the task of promoting the firm to a committee of lawyers, not a marketing department of nonlawyers.*

As noted previously, many firms have what they call their "marketing department." This department is made up of young people who may have a degree in marketing and are hired to ensure the firm is properly marketed to existing and potential clients. After that person or those persons are hired, the lawyers in the firm breathe a collective sigh of relief. They no longer have to be bothered with such a mundane task as business promotion. After all, they are lawyers!

However, the few entrepreneurial members of the firm usually ignore the marketing types and continue doing what they have always done, and that is generate business for the firm. By doing so, they put themselves in a position to demand the most money at the end of the year. The lawyers who bring in the most work make the most money and have the most influence and power in the firm. If you think law firms are apolitical, think again. The lawyer who bills the most and brings in the most legal work is more equal than the rest of the partners who do neither. Usually, lawyers who bring in the work are also very good lawyers and do a terrific job for their clients, but that is not always the case.

I believe having a marketing department composed of nonlawyers, who do not know the legal business and who have never done legal work for clients, is a feel-good waste of time designed by lawyers who probably inherited their practice from someone who retired from the firm. These lawyers bill a large sum each year as a result of riding on the coattails of a predecessor and so have no need to generate business.

In effect, these people are the beneficiaries of a practice developed by an entrepreneurial lawyer who was at the firm before them. These are the people who cause problems within a partnership. Everyone in the firm knows these lawyers gained their present position through pure luck. They are, generally speaking, legends in their own minds, constantly tooting their own horn. The true entrepreneurial lawyer can spot these phonies a mile away. They have no idea how to market their firm, so they establish a marketing department when they should be giving the task to the few entrepreneurial lawyers in their midst. They must be dealt with for the long-term benefit of a growing firm.

> ***My Advice:*** *Give the job of marketing the firm to a few entrepreneurial lawyers in your firm. The job is not all that time consuming, and a committee of two or three lawyers who are interested in promoting their firm would do a superior job. Whatever money is paid to the marketing department could be better spent on developing new, innovative ways to promote the business to new clients and maintain existing clients.*

▶ *Target your firm's advertising carefully.*

Generally speaking, advertising is not appropriate for a law firm.

A car dealer does a great deal of electronic media and print advertising in an effort to reach the mass market and sell cars—to everyone and anyone. Obviously, law firms are different. A well-run office does not, or should not, want to do legal work for everyone and anyone. Mass media is not designed for the firm I have in mind. Large firms advertise not to get legal work but to pat themselves on the back in an effort to show up their competitors and stroke their egos. Advertising really is a waste of money for these big firms, but their marketing departments probably suggested they do so.

That is not to say that advertising is all bad. It isn't. Our market area was south of a major east-west roadway and therefore convenient to a large number of people; there were hundreds of thousands of people and innumerable businesses located within our market area. Because we were basically a full-service firm, it was important to let our neighbours know that they did not have to venture downtown, fight traffic, and try to find a parking spot when they could use our services.

We were close, we would meet them on their way to work or on their way home, and we had lots of free parking. In addition, we were not precluded from doing legal work for downtown-based businesses, which we did and did successfully. Advertising was a way to educate the people in our market area about the benefits of dealing with our firm.

Most communities have monthly newsletter publications containing information, articles and notification of various events of interest to members of their community. Advertising in these publications is a very cost-effective way to let potential clients know you are there in the community and willing to do any legal work they might have.

I remember drafting an ad for such a publication. The headline of the ad was: "EVERYBODY HATES LAWYERS, until they need one!" I then went on to describe the types of legal work we did and invited readers to call lawyers in the firm who specialized in areas of the law that would appeal to the average guy. Real estate transactions, wills and estates, personal injury and corporate law were just some of the areas of the law we wanted our neighbours to know we specialized in.

My Advice: Target your advertising to potential clients in your community. Let them know you are there, and capable and willing to do any legal work they may have.

▸ **Purchase thoughtful promotional items.**

It is extremely important to keep your name and contact information easily accessible for your existing clients and to hand out your contact information to prospective clients. Promotional items are an inexpensive way to keep your firm's name in front of prospective and existing clients, and they work.

Desk calendars with your name and contact information are an example. If you want to get a bit fancier, use the months of the year to highlight various lawyers in your firm. Doing so gives you the opportunity to reinforce in your clients' eyes the type of legal work each lawyer in your firm does on a day-to-day basis. Photos of your lawyers and key support staff are a good idea. You will never, ever, have clients say they went elsewhere for a legal matter because they "didn't think you did that kind of work."

My Advice: Writing pads, pens and key chains with your name and contact information highlighted are, believe it or not, very well received, are useful for the client, keep your name front and centre and are affordable business promotional items. We used Don deForest of The Impress Corporation for ideas. Don had myriad innovative ways for us to, as he would say, "schmooze your clients." I recommend Don to you.

▶ **Send out monthly newsletters.**

Monthly newsletters are another way to keep in touch with your clients. Ideally the newsletter should address topics that are relevant to your clients. Newsletters give you an opportunity to point out changes in the law that may affect how your clients carry on business and to point out pitfalls to avoid. Newsletters reinforce in your clients' mind that you are constantly looking out for their best interests.

Nowadays, newsletters can be emailed to clients, making newsletters more convenient, economical and environmentally friendly. By adding a subscription option to your firm's website, you make it simple for people to subscribe to receive your newsletter.

The downside of newsletters is that they are time consuming and, once started, difficult to stop without losing face.

> *My Advice: If you have a couple of lawyers in your firm who have the ability to write coherently, assign them the task of preparing informative newsletters, and then make sure they do not drop the ball.*

▸ **Hold seminars on issues of interest to your clients.**

Holding seminars can be worthwhile but, like newsletters, are very time consuming. However, holding one or two seminars per year that deal with topical legal issues and to which you invite your clients reinforces in their minds that you do, in fact, have their best interests at heart. Your end goal is for your clients to believe that it is in their best interests to have your firm as THEIR lawyers.

> *My Advice: Seminars are a unique way to keep your firm's name in front of your clients when combined with other marketing initiatives.*

RULE #2

Do the work quickly, efficiently and well

▶ Clients do not want their legal matters to go to the Supreme Court of Canada. They have absolutely no desire to have their problem set legal precedent. Clients want whatever legal issue they bring to you resolved as quickly as possible and for a fee that is reasonable and of a value commensurate with the problem being resolved.

Too many lawyers turn a simple legal problem into what some refer to as a "dripping roast," equating the fat dripping from a roast cooking on a rotisserie to dollars—lots of them.

My best advice in this regard is to treat your clients like you would appreciate being treated by a professional advisor.

Another aspect of doing the work quickly, efficiently and well is technology. Today's technology can be a huge benefit to a busy lawyer—provided the technology performs as advertised and accomplishes what you expect of it. It is fundamentally important—and you must make absolutely sure—the technology you purchase is right for your practice. Avoid getting rushed into making decisions about technology purchases. A mistake can be much too disruptive, not to mention costly. Take the time to ensure that the expense you incur will have a net benefit to your practice and enhance it as well. My experience in this area may be of help.

Solving problems quickly and efficiently...

When I was in law school, we had a contracts professor by the name of Peter Cumming. Professor Cumming went on to become a justice of the Ontario Superior Court. Anyway, on his exams, he deducted marks from an answer if, before dealing with the law surrounding the problem, a practical solution was not considered at the outset.

I never forgot Professor Cumming's position in this regard. I really wanted to follow the good professor's advice and get the client's problem solved as quickly as possible. So, whenever a client brought me a problem, I always tried to settle the matter with a phone call or a letter. Sometimes I would get a practical lawyer on the other side, and the problem would be solved quickly without having to resort to formal, time-consuming and expensive legal proceedings. I really did not want to turn the problem into a "dripping roast"; it would have been very easy to do that. By solving my client's problem quickly and efficiently, the client would sing my praises from the rooftops and inevitably, new work would roll in from friends, acquaintances and extended family.

4

Structuring Your Firm

Structuring a firm like a pyramid is important for the person who starts a firm. That person signs a lease, gets a bank loan, finds clients and manages the firm's day-to-day affairs, including all the time-consuming managerial tasks. It is important that the person who does all of these things is compensated properly. Most partnerships fail because the contribution to the partnership is not fair. Invariably, one or more partners contribute more to the firm's success than the others, yet human nature is such that the noncontributing partners want to be paid the same amount as the contributing partners. Eventually that form of business organization will fail.

I am not opposed to a partnership, necessarily, but only after people have proven their worth to the firm. Readers should always remember that a true partnership is the absolute worst form of business organization ever invented by man! What really works in a law partnership is a benevolent dictatorship with an edge, where laggards actually fear for their jobs. Again, it has been my experience that people in general will do everything they think they can get away with unless held accountable. And it is my observation that things are getting worse in this regard, not better.

▶ *Create experts in fields of law through specialization.*

When I started practicing law, individual lawyers did just about every kind of legal work, from real estate transactions to criminal work and everything in between. How we avoided negligence claims is still a mystery to me.

Gradually, some lawyers (not all, by any means) decided they could be much more productive and make more money if they concentrated on, and became experts in, one or two areas of the law. Of course, the Law Society would not allow you to refer to yourself as an "expert," but de facto, you were.

In my case, I was directed into doing real estate law by the firm I was with at the time. And that was just fine with me. Real estate legal work was not all that difficult to attract. I would buy realtors lunch and attend their Monday morning meetings to point out potential problems to avoid. I was available to help them when they faced a thorny problem and needed my assistance in drafting one clause or another in a Real Estate Purchase Contract.

By the time I opened my own firm in 1980, I had pretty much specialized in real property/ banking law but not entirely. In the early days, we needed to keep the wolf from the door, so through necessity, we did everything except litigation. As our firm grew, we added lawyers who did only litigation. We then added lawyers who did Wills and Estates, Securities and Corporate Commercial law. I was adamant that specialization was the future of the practice of law, and I wanted to be ahead of the curve.

It was not always easy to convince lawyers to specialize and give up some of their clients to other members of the firm. In effect, they were afraid that if their billings slipped while developing a specialty, their income would fall. The politics of law firms gave their concerns some legitimacy. I had to think of a way to get the lawyers in my firm to buy into the idea of a firm of specialists while not causing mass paranoia. The answer was the concept of the *Originating Lawyer.*

> **My Advice:** *In the role of an expert, you are better able to concentrate your efforts in promoting business and impress potential clients with your knowledge of an area of the law in which the client needs specialized, expert help.*

Improve your influence by being an originating lawyer...

Early on with my own firm, there were several associates, but virtually all the legal work came from my clients. Knowing that relationships were key to developing a prosperous firm, I was leery of giving up my clients to lawyers who may leave and take my clients with them.

My other concern was evidenced by one of the associates who for a long time billed very little. As the work I gave him matured, his billings slowly improved. At the end of the first month, when he had actually paid for himself and had made the firm a few bucks, he came into my office and asked for a raise. He didn't get the raise, but he sure didn't lack nerve. Shortly after, this fellow left and ultimately became a partner with a big downtown firm. I was not sorry to see him go.

These two issues—giving up relationships and legal work—caused me to spend a great deal of time thinking about the problem. My solution was to develop a two-tiered billing system in which the person who did the work got credit for their billings and the person who brought the work into the office received credit as the originating lawyer. So, we had the "responsible lawyer" and the "originating lawyer."

I was of the view that all lawyers were, in theory anyway, capable of doing legal work. However, those who were able to bring work to the firm were few and far between. Accordingly, I was always more impressed with the "originating lawyer" figures when it came time to decide on raises or bonuses. What I hope readers will glean from this book is how to go about being an originating lawyer, thereby improving your influence and income within the ranks of a partnership, whether big or small.

▸ *Acknowledge the originating lawyers—the ones who bring in the work.*

Although I am sure some will claim otherwise, as far as I am aware, I was the first to implement the concept of the originating lawyer. Working with our office manager, we developed an accounting program that allowed me to know the person who brought legal work into the office (the originating lawyer) and the person who did the work (the responsible lawyer). The new accounting system would, at the end of each month, tell me how much each lawyer billed. More importantly, it showed how much of the work billed was brought to the firm and which lawyer brought in the work.

I really paid attention to who the originating lawyers were. That acknowledgement made it easier for lawyers to pass work on to others in the firm who were better suited and had more knowledge of a specific area of the law. I wanted the best people to represent our clients. It didn't always work perfectly, but if people didn't fool around with the concept, it worked well and acknowledged those who accomplished the hardest task of the practice of law—getting the work in the door.

As our firm grew, some of the lawyers (one or two in particular) started to figure out ways to beat the system. They claimed they were the originating lawyer for clients adopted or inherited from retiring partners. Everyone knew they were not the originating lawyers, but the management that succeeded me, being some of the worst offenders in this regard, did nothing to stop the cheating. A good system was made less effective because of the greedy shortsightedness of self-centred people who thought only of themselves and did not put the best interests of the law firm first.

When we first opened our office, there was only one originating lawyer: me. Virtually all work in the firm came from my clients. As a result, if I passed on work to someone, I had to be careful not to allow that person to steal my client and take a walk. I had to maintain relationships with some of my clients even if I no longer did work for them.

My Advice: One can reasonably assume that someone graduating from law school can, after some practical experience, do competent legal work. These types of people are numerous, but it's difficult to find lawyers who can do both legal work and bring work in the door. Make

> *sure to honour the lawyers who bring in legal
> work as originating lawyers, as these folks are
> worth their weight in gold to the firm.*

▸ *A partnership is the absolute worst form of business organization ever invented.*

Partnerships are based on the faulty premise that each partner will contribute to the partnership equally. Unfortunately, that just never occurs in the real world. There are partners who have a good work ethic. There are partners who have supportive spouses and those whose spouses are the tail that wags the dog. There are partners who can bring in work, and there are (but shouldn't be) partners who just do legal work that others bring in. There are partners who have inherent business acumen, and there are those who have trouble balancing their cheque books. There are partners who get to work early and stay late, and then there are those who wander in late, go to the gym at lunch, and leave early. You get the gist.

Partners all have different personalities with different approaches to the business of the practice of law. This diversity invariably causes problems, and the major problem centres around money. The guy who wants a more relaxed "life-style" (meaning he is lazy and does not want to work hard) balks when you agree, provided his percentage interest in the firm—and therefore his share of the profits—is decreased. Invariably, this type of person will cause all kinds of problems. What he really wants is to enjoy a relaxed life-style and make the same money or more. These lawyers just don't get it and are the ones who usually cause law firms to break up.

The splitting up of firm profits is, for many partners, a stressful time. Most lawyers have inflated views of their worth to a firm. It is particu-larly stressful for those who know in their hearts that their interest in the partnership should be decreased but refuse to face facts and dread hav-ing to explain to their spouses why they will take home less money the following year after their percentage interest in the firm has been reduced.

During my time at McLeod & Company, we had partners come and go, and we didn't miss any of them. Our billings and our profits continued to go up. Although I have no personal knowledge of this, I expect that after I left the firm, it did just fine and the firm's success continued. However,

I have been told that the culture of the firm has changed quite a bit and not necessarily for the better. I left a legacy of success and a template to follow for those who became future managing partners of the firm. Whether or not they followed the example I set was entirely up to them.

> *My Advice: Partnerships in the legal game are the way things are done. There may be better forms of business organization for a firm, but for the time being, this is the norm. If you have a desire to start your own firm and grow it like I did, then keep an eye on the numerous pitfalls inherent in the "worst form of business organization ever invented by man."*

Many partners, few friends...

I think I have made it clear that I was not "buddy, buddy" with members of my firm. My wife, Brenda, and I would occasionally socialize with some people in the firm, but basically we stayed at arm's length. Our friends tended to be nonlawyers. After working as hard as I did, surrounded by lawyers and legal-related matters, the last thing I wanted to do was talk law in a social setting.

However, within the law firm during law office hours, there were certain lawyers I spent more time with than others. As I noted previously, I really enjoyed— and continue to enjoy—Allan Kolinsky's company. Al is a kind and thoughtful man with a wonderful sense of humour. People do not come any better than him. I am blessed to have spent time with Al.

Bill Walker is one fine corporate, commercial and securities lawyer. In my capacity as managing partner, Bill made that role, as far as he was concerned, easy. Bill just "put his nose down and his tail up" and made a huge contribution to the firm. When I say that work ethics vary between lawyers, I was thinking of Bill. He was always the first in the office each day. I do not know for sure how early he arrived, but I do know that when I showed up around 6:30 a.m., the motor in Bill's car was cold. At the end of the day or before a long weekend, I would take a walk around the office, and Bill was always there to keep me company. Bill is a special guy who, along with his wife Donna and their daughter Julia, has literally travelled the world.

I understand that Bill recently retired from the firm. I think Bill was the best at what he did. We still have lunch together the odd time.

▶ *A formula for paying associates.*

If you want to open a firm and then tread water economically, go out into the world with two or three partners and eke out an existence. If you want to make money, follow my advice and start thinking about your firm as a pyramid, with you at the peak and everybody else, in varying degrees, below you. The base of the pyramid is composed of associates. For all intents and purposes, the associates do work that is passed down to them from those at the top.

A good rule of thumb is to pay an associate one third of what they bill and collect. The remaining two thirds goes to the firm. Of course, the two thirds helps cover part of the office overhead and contributes to partners' income. After all, it is not the lot in life for partners of a firm to provide a warm, cozy place for associates to work. Associates have an obligation to pay for themselves and generate a profit for the firm. For the partners, it's a pretty good gig, and aspiring to join the ranks of this privileged class is what keeps an associate working like a dog. It's also why, I believe, the average lady lawyer leaves the business well before her prime. I will discuss women in the law later.

My Advice: Do not make an associate a partner in your firm until that associate is bringing in enough legal work to keep two lawyers busy. Varying from that rule caused me grief.

5

HIRE THE BEST

IT GOES WITHOUT SAYING that hiring good people is key to any successful enterprise. In the legal business, hiring articling students is a form of Russian roulette. All applicants have (or are about to have) a law degree, so one can reasonably assume that the job seekers know at least some legal theory. However, knowing legal theory is but part of the equation: personality, appearance, confidence and a strong work ethic are also important.

Hiring the best people is a difficult task, especially when the applicants do not have an employment history in the field. Experienced lawyers and paralegals are somewhat easier to deal with. For example, you can check with previous employers. You will also come to know opposing lawyers and their strengths and weaknesses; if you like what a lawyer does on the other side of a file, you might try to hire that lawyer. Unfortunately, I do not have a "silver bullet" solution for hiring good people. Much of the hiring process is by trial and error, and in my case, many errors were made over the years.

▶ *Hire the best lawyers you can find, and fire the duds.*

I must admit that I was not the best at picking winners from the pool of lawyers and potential articling students. Don't get me wrong; we hired some exceedingly good lawyers, in addition to students who became lawyers and, ultimately, partners in the firm. However, we went through a "cast of thousands" to get to that point. I would joke with my partners that some of the lawyers we hired peaked at the interview and went downhill from there.

I tried everything to find the best lawyers and students. I even befriended the dean of the University of Calgary Law School. He referred a couple of students to us, and we hired them.

They may have been good students and members of the law school community, but they were not very good lawyers and were not asked to join our firm after their articles concluded.

I can remember interviewing potential lawyers and informing them that our firm was different from many of our competitors; we started work early in the morning and we worked late. By doing so, we would not have to work evenings and weekends. I also explained that the way we did things was not for everyone, but it was *our* way, and if that presented a problem for them, they should take a pass on our firm. Of course, the majority of applicants alleged that they would be a perfect fit for our firm, only to show their true colours after a few months had passed. They did not stay with the firm.

I really wanted each potential lawyer or student I interviewed to be the superstar lawyer we were always looking for. Unfortunately, I was wrong more than I was right. I hate to say this, but too many lawyers, especially some of the newer variety, look for ways to avoid hard work but expect to be compensated generously. That type of person did not last long at my firm.

My Advice: Honestly, I have no words of wisdom to point you in the right direction. I expect that you will experience the same thing we did. Some of the people you hire will be terrific, and others will not. Whatever you do, get rid of those who will not make your firm better. Bad or lazy lawyers will cause you nothing but grief and will very quickly undo all your hard work in attracting clients and growing your firm. The practice of law is hard work, especially if you perform the task conscientiously and in a timely manner.

Expect the unexpected...

My pal and former partner Bill Walker was provided with a copy of my manuscript for this book, and although he was probably just being kind, he said he enjoyed reading the document. However, he suggested I add this particular heading—Expect the Unexpected—and then went on to remind me of an incident involving a lawyer we had hired in our corporate securities department.

I do not think I hired this particular guy, but I could have. I did not work with him as he was in a different department of the firm. However, I do remember walking by his office on too many occasions and observing him with his feet up on his desk (really, one of my desks), chatting away on the phone. I had the urge to knock his feet off the desk, but restrained myself.

Anyway, this guy was a con man. Fortunately, he had been with our firm for only a very short while before he announced he was leaving to join a highly respected large downtown Calgary law firm. A week or so after he had left our firm, he called and asked for his job back, because, he alleged, the bigger firm had misled him in regard to the type of work he would be doing. We actually considered taking him back, but as the legal community in Calgary at that time was close-knit, it didn't take long to learn the truth. This fellow had been fired by the downtown firm almost before he started. The big firm had performed its due diligence and discovered that this guy had doctored his transcripts to substantially increase his grades and his academic awards.

Of course, we did not hire him back, and he was ultimately dealt with by the Law Society of Alberta. Although I am not sure, something tells me that our "kinder and gentler" Law Society ultimately allowed this guy to be reinstated. In the old days, he would have been disbarred and never, ever allowed back as a member of the Law Society of Alberta or any other provincial law society for that matter. Things have changed.

▸ *Hire the best personnel, and pay them well.*

It is obvious that legal secretaries and paralegals are important to a successful lawyer and to a legal practice. Excellent legal assistants are not easy to find, so when you find one, pay her or him very well. An assistant can make you look smarter than you are and much more efficient than you could ever be with just an average or below-average assistant. The best assistants are the ones with years of experience, but experience is not always a reliable criterion. While you should do your best to check an applicant's background, it was my experience that previous employers were hesitant to give a negative reference. The result is that when you hire an assistant, you take your chances.

One thing is certain; it will not take you very long to know what you have hired.

It was my observation as well that some applicants who alleged they had legal experience must have gained that experience by dating a lawyer. It quickly became apparent if the new employee was any good. Try to negotiate a probationary period with the new hire. Don't be afraid to use legal secretarial employment services, and try to develop a rapport with those folks. If you develop a good relationship with personnel experts, they can save you a great deal of time and money. The fees they charge, and the guarantees they provide, make using these agencies well worthwhile and more economical than doing the job yourself. However, as you get larger and hire an office manager, the task of hiring support staff could be one of his or her responsibilities.

We recognized the need to develop really good legal assistants, so we instituted a senior/junior legal-assistant program. Young people who had taken the legal-assistant course at one of the facilities of higher learning but lacked practical experience would be teamed up with more experienced paralegals. This program allowed us to train our own staff to do things the way we wanted them done. As senior legal assistants moved on, we filled the vacancy with one of our juniors. This idea was put forward by our office manager Betty Tweedie, and notwithstanding the usual protests from the anti-change partners, she had my support. We adopted her idea, and it worked really well. You see, some partners were negative influences on the firm and usually opposed most new or innovative ideas. However, they were not the ones with the responsibility of running a law firm; I was.

Legal assistants are just some of the employees a firm will require. Knowledgeable accounting personnel are an absolute necessity. You must pay a great deal of attention to trust-account accounting; make sure you hire someone you can trust and who has the capability to do anything and everything required by the Law Society. Getting on the wrong side of the Law Society accounting requirements is a very bad thing and will cause you nothing but grief if you do not follow their rules to the letter.

Many lawyers get into trouble by trying to do some of the accounting while also doing legal work. You would be much further ahead to pay yourself less and a good bookkeeper/accounting person more. I cannot stress enough the importance of first-class accounting assistance. You want to be able to sleep at night.

Finally, it is just too commonplace for firms of all kinds to pay their receptionists less than any other employee. What a mistake!

The receptionist is the first person with whom a potential client speaks. If that primary contact person answers the telephone in an unprofessional manner, butchers the Queen's English, leaves a caller on hold or doesn't greet clients in a friendly manner, you are defeating all of the other good things you may be doing for your clients. Not having a good receptionist can scuttle the really hard work of getting clients in the first place.

It's a funny thing, but after having just written the preceding paragraph, Brenda and I attended my old firm to have our revised wills signed. I approached the receptionist, introduced Brenda and myself, and advised that we were there for an appointment with Roy Klassen. (Roy heads up the firm's Wills and Estates and Estate Planning Department and is an excellent lawyer.) Within mere seconds of giving the receptionist this information, we overheard her advising a completely different lawyer that we were there and identifying us by totally incorrect names. In fact, the names she gave were not even close to our actual names. So, here you have a situation where a very good lawyer, who has done excellent work for us, has that excellence depreciated by some bird-brained receptionist. A receptionist like this should be dealt with so that future damage to the firm will be avoided, and the sooner, the better.

During my tenure, for the most part, we had excellent receptionists who looked professional, had a great telephone manner, recognized the voices of the clients for whom we did large amounts of work, helped organize firm lunches and receptions, and when not out-of-control busy (which they usually were), did all kinds of collateral tasks to benefit our firm.

> *My Advice: Employees are key to your success. Take the time to find the right ones and then treat those folks really well. You will be glad you did.*

▶ **The challenges of addressing gender and minority equality within the firm.**

When I went to law school, there were, I think, two hundred and forty first-year students. After three years of law school, two hundred and fifteen of us graduated, and of that number, eighteen were female. Since that time, the number of women attending law school has increased dramatically. Currently, the number of women attending law school exceeds the number of men.

In an effort to be politically correct, various governments started fast-tracking women to positions on provincial and federal courts. We were told that it was imperative that members of our courts be representative of the Canadian population in terms of gender, colour, ethnicity and religion. In fact, our liberal friends at the Canadian Bar Association (CBA) jumped at the opportunity to prepare gender-related reports; the conclusions drawn from these reports were used to influence law societies across Canada. Those various law societies then instructed their members to follow these new rules. Law firms were now prohibited from asking questions during interviews that an interviewee might find sexist and therefore offensive.

As I recall, a CBA commission was formed, with Supreme Court of Canada Justice Bertha Wilson at the helm. The purpose of the commission was to investigate gender equality (really gender *inequality*) within the legal profession. The suspicion was that the white-male-dominated profession was holding women and minorities back from advancing within large-firm partnerships—the infamous "glass ceiling." In effect, females and minorities were being discriminated against by "old white guys." The committee had many people come forward and relate their personal experiences—or at least their perception of their experiences—of how they had been treated.

I remember certain female Calgary lawyers being involved in this commission and traveling to and from eastern Canada on a regular basis to work on this initiative. It was my observation that these ladies had a pretty good idea of what the Commission's conclusions should be even before they got involved. Perhaps I was wrong, but when the Commission's report became public, it stated that—surprise, surprise—women and minorities were, in fact, discriminated against by the big boy, white-male-dominated law firms.

Law societies embraced the report's findings and soon started advising firms on how best to conduct their hiring practices to avoid the continuance of this blatant discrimination. In fact, the Law Society of Alberta created a Gender Equality Ombudsman, and lawyers who felt aggrieved were encouraged to get in touch with this person, who was, of course, a woman.

As I have noted throughout this book, I considered myself an entrepreneur who just happened to be a lawyer. In that capacity, I wrote the Law Society and told them that I disagreed with the Commission's findings and their implementation of rules which governed how I was to now go about hiring or firing lawyers or students. In fact,

I told them that their new directives insulted me as a businessman. I asked them: why in the world would I fire a lawyer who was a really good lawyer, one who worked very hard, just because that person happened to be a woman or a member of a minority? It just did not make sense to me that anyone in management would be so stupid. What did make sense to me was the inability of incompetent lawyers to look in a mirror and accept the fact that they were fired, not because they were members of a minority group, but simply because they were just plain lazy and very poor lawyers. It was easier to blame their incompetence on gender or ethnicity. Of course, that was not what these folks wanted to hear, and they had a powerful ally in the form of the various law societies and the politically correct folks at the CBA.

Of course, we hired women and members of minority groups to work at our firm, and some became partners. However, the really practical problem I had as the person tasked with the responsibility of running our firm—and a problem that probably hadn't even entered the minds of those who championed this gender-equality business—was what the hell was I to do when a female lawyer came into my office to announce that she was pregnant? Of course, I had to appear excited and pleased—and in a way I was—but I also had an overwhelming feeling of concern for our clients and our firm. What would I do with the clients this lawyer was handling? Could I find someone to take over her files? Or would I just have to increase the workload of other lawyers in her department? What was I going to do? This was a problem I did not need. It was, frankly, a moment of real concern for me.

We survived several similar maternity leave episodes, but now, new mothers had new responsibilities at home, ones that didn't exist before. As a result, they were not able to get to the office as early as they once did, and they could not stay as late. They wanted, understandably, to have flex hours. They wanted to come and go as they pleased and, in effect, leave it to me to deal with upset clients who could not reach their lawyers. This did not make my life easier as the firm's managing partner.

I tell you this, along with all the background, so that you understand the practical struggles we encountered when accommodating new parents in our firm. We did our best to be fair and reasonable with all lawyers, to stay within the confines of the law, and more importantly, to do the right thing in each circumstance. In this new world of ours, you will be required to do even more, but it will not be easy. Don't kid yourself. You will need to deal with extended leave for both new mothers and fathers, flex time, balancing workloads—and one more question that we didn't expect but is still an issue today. At the end of the year, some lawyers who had family obligations that took them away from the office became upset when their contemporaries, who had both worked and billed many more hours, were paid more money.

What has happened recently is that women lawyers have formed their own firms. They are able to deal with the practical problems with which female lawyers are faced in a much better and more understanding manner than I ever could. These ladies should still read this book.

One last thing: as I recall, the Bertha Wilson report noted that the average female lawyer stays in the legal business for 3.2 years or some length of time like that. They get married, start families and have new, more important priorities than the practice of law. Chances are they married someone in the legal or other profession, making it unnecessary economically for them to work.

In effect, they retire for the time being, and who can blame them? The legal game is hard, and it is demanding. If you do not have to be involved in such a pressure-packed business, why would any reasonable person do so?

> *My Advice: It can be safely said that my comments in this area are not politically correct. When you are required to make decisions that are for the benefit or even survival of your firm, do what you think is right, and let common sense be your guide while always keeping the best interests of the firm in mind.*

6

THE DAY-TO-DAY
MANAGEMENT
OF THE FIRM

MANAGING LAWYERS is an almost impossible task, one that ultimately resulted in my early and premature retirement. Too many lawyers have the belief that they are smarter than everyone else, making them incapable of being managed. The fact is that some of the dumbest people I have met in my life are members of the legal community. Don't get me wrong; there are many more really smart, community minded, hardworking, decent people populating the ranks of the legal profession, but there are just too many lawyers who are, in my view, seriously flawed. If you doubt that statement, have a visit with the Chair of any provincial law society's Conduct Committee and have your eyes opened.

The oft-used expression of trying to "herd cats" is an appropriate description of what it's like to manage lawyers. It is an assignment bordering on the impossible.

However, when you start a firm and you are the managing partner, managing is what you must do. The day-to-day management of the firm means trying to arrive at decisions that balance what everyone wants with the best interests of the firm. It means dealing with everything from filing systems to ethics—ensuring that everyone in the firm lives up to the highest standards expected of legal professionals.

Managing the firm also means dealing with technology. It is fundamentally important to provide the lawyers and support staff in your firm with all the tools necessary for them to complete the legal work required by the clients of the firm as efficiently and as quickly as is reasonably possible.

Today, things move at what amounts to an unreasonably demanding speed in virtually all industries. The legal business is not exempt. In order to effectively compete, it is fundamentally important that the very best technology available is utilized to enhance your firm's performance of legal services.

When I finally got tired of herding cats, I mean, lawyers...

The person who coined the phrase "herding cats" must have had some, but not all, of the lawyers in my firm in mind.

One fellow started to feel his oats because his personal injury practice began to bear fruit. His monthly billings increased dramatically, and he made darn sure everyone in the firm knew it. When convenient— which was always—he neglected to appreciate that the solicitors in the firm had provided the cash flow necessary for him, and others in his cabal of followers, to pay the disbursements necessary to carry on a personal injury practice. Our firm was paid a fee equal to a percentage of the recovery if successful, usually around thirty percent, but nothing if the claim was unsuccessful. However, the dirty truth is that any contingency fee lawyer seldom, if ever, takes a case where liability is an issue. They take only cases where liability is clear and the only question to be answered is how much the injured party will receive in compensation.

This particular lawyer had developed relationships with some chiropractors who referred "patients" to him. As far as I know, there was no quid pro quo, but to be honest, I often wondered.

In any event, this lad started feeling his oats, and he and a small group around him started working at cross purposes to long-established firm policies. I could have made an issue of the game this guy was playing, and because he was not well-liked by the majority of lawyers in the firm, I probably could have dealt with him. However, at that point, as I mentioned earlier, I had grown weary of both the practice and the task of managing the firm. So, to avoid ongoing annoyances, I decided it was time for me to retire, which I did.

▶ *Strive for consensus, but be prepared to make a decision if consensus cannot be reached in a reasonable amount of time.*

As noted, lawyers are almost impossible to manage effectively. Generally speaking, they are of above-average intelligence, but the vast majority have zero business sense. Those that do have some business acumen are difficult to manage; in our firm, they would exert their self-importance by fighting every innovation that I and our office manager would suggest. Although I always tried my best to get consensus and listen to all points of view, when all the talking was done, someone had to make a decision. I made no qualms about describing myself as a "benevolent dictator." This was a firm I had started—a firm I had given everything I had to make it a success. If the firm should ever fail—and I was hell bent on that never happening—it was going to be the result of something I did and not others in the firm. I always harkened back to when the firm started and my partner of the day darn near bankrupted us before we got started. It was a lesson I would not soon forget, and I was going to be sure to make our firm a success or die in the process.

My Advice: Try to reach consensus on decisions. If that doesn't work, be prepared to step in and make a decision. I felt that sometimes a bad decision was better than maintaining an ineffective status quo.

▶ *Encourage lawyers to specialize in areas of law that play to their strengths and not their weaknesses.*

Early on in the firm's development, we hired a lawyer who was just slightly junior to me. The lawyer had been in a two-person partnership that was, when he approached us, in serious financial difficulties and teetering on bankruptcy. We hired the guy, and he brought with him a variety of clients.

This fellow had a pleasing personality but was, as evidenced by his financial state of affairs, not a very good businessman. He continued to want to do a generalist type of practice even though that was not what I wanted. I kept badgering him and, as noted previously, instituted the originating lawyer concept so he would more readily pass certain files on to others who specialized in the area of law required by the client.

Because of this guy's pleasing personality and built-in empathy for virtually all things, I suggested he consider specializing in the area of Wills and Estates. I explained to him that demographics clearly showed that, as Baby Boomers grew older, Wills and Estates was going to be a fast-growing area of the law. To his credit, he took on the challenge and eventually became one of the best Wills and Estate lawyers in the Province of Alberta, if not all of Western Canada. His billings followed suit, and not only did he develop a good-sized department within the law firm, his prestige and clout within the firm were enhanced. Tragically, he recently died of cancer after fighting the disease for several years.

> *My Advice: Allow for and encourage specialization in various areas of law. Be aware of new opportunities for business, and suggest areas of specialization that are a good fit for lawyers and that will also increase billings for the firm.*

▶ *Always do the right thing without compromise.*

If you are inherently unethical, and if other lawyers cannot trust you, you are in for a very unpleasant career. Lawyers rely on undertakings given by one to the other. Most are in writing and speak for themselves. Others are verbal; an opposing lawyer may innocently rely on that verbal undertaking and, based on that, take steps on behalf of a client. If the person giving the undertaking reneges on the deal and in doing so causes the lawyer who acted on the undertaking—and that lawyer's client—grief or monetary loss, the offending lawyer has just caused himself a world of future problems. The victimized lawyer will tell everyone at his firm and anyone else who will listen that a particular lawyer cannot be trusted.

During my days of practice, I ran into some lawyers who could not be relied upon to live up to a verbal undertaking. As a result, everything—and I mean everything—was confirmed in writing to those particular lawyers. Fortunately, these guys were in a minority, but there were far too many for my liking. And some, surprisingly, were senior lawyers who should have known better.

The Law Society of Alberta has an Ethics Committee, which is now called the Professional Responsibility Committee. The committee is composed of a couple of Benchers and representatives of the profession. That committee deals with ethical issues that arise from time to time, primarily between lawyers. For example, one lawyer may complain to the committee about what another lawyer had or had not done. If the offending lawyer's actions were deemed to be egregious and contrary to The Code of Professional Conduct, that lawyer could be referred to the Conduct Committee, and the consequences could be most unpleasant for the offending lawyer. The aforesaid Code of Professional Conduct is, simply stated, a comprehensive guide that governs the conduct of lawyers within a particular jurisdiction.

I was a member of both the Professional Responsibility and the Conduct committees, and one thing I noticed was that the same names kept popping up time and time again. As such, it was never a surprise to see these people eventually disbarred. Today, however, I am not sure what offence you must commit to get bounced out of the profession. A lawyer was found guilty by a Conduct Panel of forging a judge's signature on a formal Court document, and nothing of substance happened to that lawyer.

I read about a recent case in which a criminal lawyer acting on behalf of a drug dealer took money that the drug dealer had forfeited to the Court and arranged to have the funds paid out of Court to his firm. The funds were deposited into the law firm's general account. You might say that's okay, as the drug dealer probably owed the lawyer for the services provided. However, those would not be the facts of this case. The lawyer had been paid in full for representing the drug dealer. The funds in question were sitting in Court, having been forfeited to the Crown with the stipulation by the Crown that the money not be returned to the drug dealer. The drug dealer's lawyer decided to apply to the Court for the release of the funds, and the application was approved. The funds were sent, by mail as I recall, to the lawyer's firm, and the lawyer's partner deposited the cheque in the firm's general account and divided up the money between the two partners.

The Conduct Committee that heard this matter did not find that the law firm had done anything wrong. This conclusion was rather astonishing, as the funds were clearly not owed to the law firm. The firm's partners converted the funds to their own use, even though they clearly were not entitled to them. In any event, the unethical lawyer and his partner were unjustly enriched. However, the Panel found no wrongdoing based on a technicality any reasonable person would have difficulty understanding.

If you would like your eyes opened to the unbelievable stupidity of some lawyers—even after six years of university and one year of articles—log on to any provincial law society's website and click on "Hearings." You will be amazed at what some of these people have done to get into trouble with their governing bodies. In the '60s, '70s and '80s, these lawyers would have been disbarred quickly. Today, I am not sure what a lawyer must do to get kicked out of the profession. As in virtually all things these days, it seems no one is ever called to account. A "kinder and gentler" Law Society to be sure, but a better one? I think not.

> *My Advice: In life—but especially as a lawyer—you are only as good as your reputation. Respect it. Live it. Never compromise your principles. Live up to your word. Always do the right thing without compromise. Have your colleagues say that you are a trusted, ethical lawyer of the highest degree. By making your word your bond, your interaction with other lawyers will make your life as a lawyer much easier.*

▶ **If necessary, forcefully encourage your lawyers to be innovative and organized!**

Our firm grew quickly, and our file load increased at the same pace. We were busy and getting busier. I noticed that finding any particular file quickly was becoming difficult, if not bordering on impossible.

Of course, each file tab was printed with the name of the client and the subject matter of the file, but the files blurred together given their similar colour. In addition, we had started doing some litigation work and some personal injury litigation. These files were "organized" by using a very large, copper-covered peg. Each piece of paper was attached to the peg, located on the top left-hand corner of the file. Correspondence, police reports, medical information, pleadings and everything else were attached to this one peg. Lawyers working on the file, or familiarizing themselves with the file, had to rummage through everything on the tab. It was a backward system, and I wanted it changed.

I asked our office manager if she would get in touch with the company we purchased our files from to see if they would manufacture for us a variety of coloured, multi-tabbed files. Now, I acknowledge that there were files available with more than one tab, but these files were usually green in colour and did not have nearly the number of tabs I had in mind.

The file manufacturing company was very accommodating. We were able to have them make us files with a wide colour selection and with multiple tabs. The old litigation files now had a separate tab for correspondence, police reports, pleadings, medical information and any other heading that made sense. The colour picked for litigation was green. Real estate files were red and had tabs for check lists, title searches, the Real Estate Purchase Contract, correspondence and encumbrances, to name a few. Corporate Commercial files were blue, and so on.

This idea was presented to my partners, and to my astonishment, I got pushback. I was given all kinds of reasons as to why they preferred their old system. However, none of their concerns made any sense to me. Betty Tweedie and I tried to point out the benefits to the efficient maintenance of files, and although some understood and were supportive, some, for whatever reason, continued their opposition. Finally, I had had enough. Anyone could see that our proposal made perfect sense. I announced that they were to get busy and have their secretaries start the conversion process, which was to be completed by the end of the month.

Although some of the more vociferous opponents complied sulkily, it was not long before even the loudest opponent admitted that the new file system made their lives much easier. There was no interest in returning to the old ways. The amazing part of this story to me was that some people did not embrace this idea right away, when originally proposed. Perhaps it was because it was not their idea.

> **My Advice:** *We would have waited for a very long time for an idea from other members of the firm that would have improved our firm's day-to-day functioning. To have waited for consensus on our proposal would have resulted in a long wait as well. If you see a better way of doing things, just do it!*

▶ **Annual retreats are an efficient way to meet with all members of the firm.**

Once our firm got to a reasonable size where, as we once joked, we no longer had room to meet in the firm's washroom, annual retreats were organized in various locations in Alberta.

During the retreat, the partners would meet on a Friday night to review various matters affecting the firm, including all financial issues. Many times, Betty was invited to the Friday meetings to explain various things she and I were proposing.

Saturday was devoted to meeting with all members of the firm to go over many of the matters discussed in this book. I am sure that, after a while, the *spiel* became boring, especially for the veterans. Regardless of the boredom factor, I thought it a good idea to restate the firm's goals and procedures.

Following the meeting, we would all gather again for dinner. There was always free time during the Saturday afternoon.

My Advice: Organize annual retreats for the firm as an efficient way to discuss matters affecting the firm, make decisions and at the same time, celebrate the firm's successes over the past year.

The flip side of annual retreats...

It's a funny thing, but you can tell a great deal about people by how they conduct themselves when invited to charge various expenses, such as when we held our annual retreats. Some people are frugal, some are reasonable, and some take advantage and charge everything and anything they can think of to their room. This latter group, albeit in the minority, are the "takers" in our midst. Everyone reading this has met this type of person at one time or another.

After I saw their inflated expenses, I didn't soon forget. I know I sound mean and vindictive, and looking back, I guess I was. However, when it came to taking advantage of the firm's generosity, the behaviour of some was the antithesis of how I thought and acted. I couldn't understand why people would not treat the firm and the firm's resources with the same reverence I did.

▸ *When it comes to office technology, be a follower, not a leader.*

Some of my former partners will argue that I was a dinosaur when it came to embracing new technology for our firm. Remembering that I retired in 2004, computer technology was, at that time, relatively new. In fact, it wasn't that long ago that I, along with some of the guys at Mason & Company, watched in awe as we received a fax from another law firm. In those days, fax machines were cutting edge when it came to office technology.

Basic computers soon followed, and computer manufacturers saw law firms as an obvious market. The lawyers at Mason & Company, wanting to be progressive and ahead of the curve, bought a Burrows computer. It was the size of a large photocopier, and our accountant hated it. It turned out to be a complete disaster, ultimately resulting in us having to retain lawyers to sue Burrows, which we did successfully. In those days, lawyers did things for one another and did so gratuitously. I recall that we bought the firm that represented us in the Burrows litigation an expensive painting in lieu of paying them a fee. Quite a civilized way of doing things that, sadly, no longer exists.

A classmate of mine worked for a large Toronto law firm. During the mid to late 1970s, that firm spent more than a million dollars on what was marketed as a state-of-the-art computer system specially designed to dramatically improve the efficiency and profitability of the firm. It, too, turned out to be a complete disaster.

I learned a lesson from the experiences of Mason & Company and my friend's Toronto law firm; I determined that computer assistance would be a good thing, provided it worked. I decided that my firm, at least in this particular area, would follow and not lead.

Our office manager, Betty Tweedie, who was one smart lady and a terrific office manager, utilized the DOS-based program WordPerfect because she was of the view that what our office needed was top-quality word processing. The program also did what we needed for all of our accounting requirements, including trust account accounting, which was really important to both myself and The Law Society of Alberta.

My preference for following rather than leading in technology did not mean that we refrained from looking at computers and computer programs that might assist our practice. I recall taking a hard look at the latest Apple hardware and software. We came very close to adopting their product, at least until Betty gave me a memo pointing out the reasons why we should not purchase the Apple system but should stick with the tried-and-true system we were presently using. I agreed with Betty's analysis, and in the face of howls of protest from some of the self-perceived captains of industry within our firm, we kept the DOS-based WordPerfect system until such time as we absolutely outgrew the capabilities of what for us had been a wonderful system that suited our needs perfectly.

Some of the lawyers in our firm were, if nothing else, persistent. I referred to them as the "Energizer bunnies." Notwithstanding their complaints about not having their own computers, I was determined to make sure whatever system we ultimately purchased worked and did what its promoters said it would do. Changing our system was a huge undertaking that most lawyers in the firm did not have to deal with. Betty and I had the problem of integrating an entirely new system into a firm structure which, by that time, had fifty support staff and more than twenty-five lawyers. After a period of time and some really hard work, we successfully moved to a computer program complete with new hardware for all lawyers, secretaries and accounting personnel. It was a difficult task to make the transition while continuing to do our work in an extremely busy law practice. The success of the conversion was a credit to Betty and our entire secretarial and accounting staff.

My Advice: When it comes to expensive technology, do not lead the pack. Make absolutely sure the technology does what you want it to do before putting the financial viability of your firm at risk.

▶ *Make sure the lawyers and staff have the best technology that is also tried and true, and helps make your law practice more efficient and profitable.*

Lawyers, being the way they are, simply cannot stay away from emails, social media and their gadgets. From the days when we looked in awe at a facsimile transmission to today, things have changed dramatically, including my opinion. We know the technology works, and it is now not state of the art but an absolute necessity. Today, if I were still the managing partner, in addition to desktop computers, lawyers would have available to them every device that makes the practice of law more efficient and profitable.

The funny thing is that lawyers are now working twenty-four hours a day because their curiosity will not allow them to park their iPhones or iPads even when they are on holidays, out for dinner with their families, or playing golf. If these people kept track of their time when dealing with client problems that show up on their devices, their firms should benefit from increased billings on a per lawyer basis. But what is the price to be paid? The lawyers who worked for me now have their wish, and I can't help but wonder how they—and their wives or husbands—like being on call at all times.

> *My Advice: Provided the new technology works, give your lawyers, especially young lawyers, all the technology they can handle within reason—their billings will increase well beyond the associated costs.*

▶ **Communicating frequently with your clients is very important.**

Busy lawyers have, literally, hundreds of files, but the average client has only one: theirs. As a result, the client's file is the most important file to that person. If the client places a call to a lawyer, the reason for the call is of utmost importance to the client. It follows therefore, that the client will be upset—and understandably so—if the call is not returned or at least acknowledged in a prompt manner.

Most people require the services of a lawyer for basic services such as having a Will prepared or closing a house purchase or sale. However, if a legal issue of more substance is involved, the experience is not normally pleasant for a client.

In fact, litigation is extremely stressful for the average person, so keeping a client informed on a continual basis and in effect, holding the client's hand through the process, are fundamentally important to maintaining a healthy solicitor/client relationship.

When I started practicing, it was important to copy clients with correspondence sent to opposing counsel, when appropriate. Many times it was a battle to get lawyers to do that. Today, with the popularity of email, texting and other forms of instant communication, only the laziest and most backward-thinking lawyers will not keep their clients fully informed.

> ***My Advice:*** *With today's various forms of communication available to lawyers, there is absolutely no excuse not to keep a client completely up to date regarding what is happening on the client's file. Doing so will reduce a lot of stress for the client.*

7

Always Make Decisions in the Best Interests of the Firm

Making a decision based on the best interests of the firm is an absolute must. I insisted on including a clause in our Partnership Agreement that stated that if a partner left the firm and competed with the firm within two years and within a certain geographic area, that partner would forfeit his or her capital account. We calculated capital accounts by adding together cash in the bank, incurred but unbilled disbursements, furniture and equipment at depreciated book value, and accounts receivable ninety days and under, and then deducted any bank debt.

Because of my ultra-conservative approach to managing the firm's affairs, we seldom had debt. When we did incur bank debt for large equipment purchases or leasehold improvements, we paid the debt off quickly. As a result, the balances of our capital accounts were impressively high, and for the longest time, the balance of my capital account was highest. At the time we entered into our Partnership Agreement, the balance of my capital account was substantially higher than the others because my percentage interest in the partnership was the largest. Accordingly, if I left the firm, I had the most to lose.

I insisted on that particular clause for the best interest of the firm. I was an advocate of the free flow of files within the office, meaning that I wanted legal work done by the lawyer possessing the expertise to do the work. However, a free flow of files would never work if a lawyer who passed a client to another member of the firm feared losing that client. If a lawyer were to leave, I did not want to see the clients I had referred to that lawyer leave as well, without that lawyer compensating the firm for the loss of a client or clients. So the deal was, leave if you want, but understand there is a price to be paid.

The above policy is an example of putting the firm first. The firm was sacred. We had a large number of people dependant on us for their jobs and their family's well-being. I was not going to jeopardize the firm or the firm's success if I could help it.

► *Getting the work sometimes means infringing on your personal space.*

Telephone directories, such as the Yellow Pages and white pages, were somewhat useful but rudimentary marketing instruments of the day, and I wanted our lawyers listed in the white pages, complete with their home phone numbers. Some of the lawyers opposed the idea of listing home phone numbers as well as office numbers. They explained that their spouses did not want people calling them at home and disrupting their lives. My question back to them was: Does your spouse enjoy eating?

We were in a pure service business, and getting legal work was not easy. I was adamant that we would use every tool available to us to get work in the door and survive as a firm. To complain about getting phone calls at home from clients or potential clients who wanted to pay us to do their legal work spoke volumes to me about those lawyers. They put the firm in a secondary position.

The Yellow Pages were another matter. They were full of lawyer ads to the point of becoming meaningless, and to advertise in the Yellow Pages was stupidly expensive. However, it was the only marketing plan many of our competitors employed. Other than to list our names and phone numbers, we did not use the Yellow Pages.

> *My Advice: Use every tool available to get the work in the door—even if it means receiving phone calls at home—and always put "the firm" first.*

▸ **Trust your gut instincts about a person's sense of ethics; the story of the expensive dress.**

One of our lawyers once brushed up against a painted wall when we were having work done to our premises. She got paint on her dress, and after taking it to the dry cleaners, she stated that the paint would not come out. She marched into

Betty's office and demanded that Betty have the painter pay for her dress because he had not put up a sign warning people of the freshly painted wall. While this was probably a pretty good legal analysis of the situation, I told Betty not to ask the painter to pay the $75.00 but to tell the lawyer if she felt that strongly about the matter she could come and see me.

The next thing I knew the lawyer was in my office, pleading her case. I asked her if she was serious. I pointed out that the painter was doing his job and in all probability was not making much money per hour. I noted that of all the people coming and going through our office, she was the only one who walked into the painted wall. However, I told her if she felt that strongly about the matter, I would buy her a new dress. She would have had to be a complete idiot not to see that I was angry.

Lo and behold, the very next day, Betty came into my office and presented me with an invoice given to her by the lawyer. I told Betty to give this lawyer a cheque for the $75.00.

Let me tell you something. That dress turned out to be the most expensive dress ever made. When it came time for a raise, bonus or a partnership, I did not forget this incident. Although this lawyer is no longer with the firm, one of my regrets is that I allowed her to continue as a member of our firm while I was the managing partner. I had more complaint calls from clients about this particular lawyer than all other lawyers in the firm combined. A lawyer in the litigation department who was more concerned about the size of a lawyer's billings rather than the quality of a lawyer's work protected her. I could have insisted and prevailed, but the fact I did not do that is a real regret of mine. As noted, the firm finally got rid of this lawyer. She detracted from the reputation of the firm.

> **My Advice:** *If a member of the firm does not mesh with the firm's values or work ethic, you may need to let that person go. Also, if an interviewee doesn't appear to have the same values as your firm, whatever you do, don't hire that person. They will not change.*

▸ **Some people are not cut out to be team players.**

Two lawyers in our Corporate, Commercial, Securities department wanted to go on vacation at the same time. These two were both senior and represented fifty percent of the lawyers in that department. I asked both of them to reconsider; I was worried that the absence of half of the lawyers in that department for two or three weeks could cause grief and put an unfair burden on Bill Walker, who was the most senior guy in the department.

My request was refused, and like the "dress" issue, I made it clear to both of these guys that I was not pleased. I felt that they were thinking more of themselves than they were of the firm. They both went anyway. After all, they argued, they were professionals and should have the autonomy to do what they wanted, when they wanted.

While they were away, Bill Walker had an emergency appendectomy. The two "vacationers" were made aware of the situation, but neither returned to the office to help out. I never forgot that. Clearly, they were not thinking of the best interests of the firm.

My Advice: All you can do is hope that members of the firm will be team players. If they are not, express your displeasure when people go

*against the values and best interests of the firm
and other employees.*

▶ **Inappropriate behaviour should not be
tolerated at any level.**

I don't think I am a prude, but there is one area
of interoffice behaviour that I could never condone: married lawyers having relationships with
secretaries or other lawyers or articling students.

The first time I remember coming across such
a situation was at Mason & Company when a new
secretary arrived. The word was that we were
doing a favour for another firm. A prominent
lawyer was having an affair with the secretary,
and the relationship became known to the lawyer's wife. His wife wanted, for understandable
reasons, the secretary to be released from the
employ of her husband's firm. Her forced departure resulted in the naughty lawyer getting in
touch with the senior guys at our firm to provide
a landing spot for the secretary. I thought this
rather underhanded; the offending lawyer pla-
cated his wife by giving the impression he had
cut all ties with the woman. In fact, he had fired
her while fully intending to continue the affair.
The firm I was with appeared quite willing to

provide the cover this lawyer needed to continue his extramarital affair.

When I had my own firm, I made it clear that inappropriate behaviour, in speech or action, would not be tolerated at any level. My reasoning was that not only did clandestine relationships harm families, they caused ongoing grief when discovered. If it is revealed that a lawyer is having an affair with another lawyer or an employee of the firm, and that relationship is allowed to continue after a family has been blown apart, what do you think will be going on in the minds of other spouses when advised by their lawyer spouses that they must work late or go to the office on the weekend? The lawyer may be as pure as the driven snow, but his or her spouse will be suspicious of a firm culture that allows extramarital relationships to exist without the offending parties being held to account.

I made it clear that the price to be paid for conduct that was unacceptable to the firm (and distasteful to me personally) was for both sides of the relationship to be fired. As I noted above, I am not a prude, but neither was I about to condone behaviour that would have a detrimental effect on the functioning of our office. Every decision made must be in the best interests of the firm. It is clearly not in the firm's best interest to be quiet about a situation that can do nothing but cause everyone grief.

I can say that, as far as I am aware, no inter-office hanky-panky occurred during my role as office manager. As a result, I never had to deal with such a problem.

However, after I had retired, I heard that two of the partners in the firm had extramarital affairs. One was with an articling student, and the other was with an employee in the firm's accounting department. Both partners had long-standing marriages and several children of various ages. Of course, these events caused serious problems for the firm and the spouses involved. In one case, the affair resulted in a divorce and the partner getting married to the student. The second situation was messier, if that is possible. The accounting employee left the firm and the relationship, and the offending partner returned to his wife and family with his tail between his legs.

All parties involved would have been summarily dismissed had I been the managing partner. In the first example above, the partner and his new wife continue to this day to be part of the firm.

Both may even be partners, another situation that I would never have allowed.

I can't help but wonder how this behaviour has affected other husband/wife relationships.

> *My Advice: It is my view that people who pull such a stunt should not necessarily be judged by me, but at the same time, they should not be allowed to leave "firm" chaos in their wake without paying a price. Had these "affairs" happened on my watch, both participants would have been summarily fired, not because they upset my moral outlook on things, but because getting rid of them was in the best long-term interest of the firm.*

▸ **The lawyers in your firm must dress to look the part their clients expect them to play.**

Like it or not, lawyers have a certain image in the minds of the general population. That image has been enhanced and perpetuated in the movies and on television. I believe most clients expect their lawyers to look the part and present themselves in a manner that does not raise eyebrows.

A lawyer cannot go before a Justice of the Court of Queen's Bench for matters other than

Chambers applications without being gowned in a black robe, a formal wing-collared white shirt, a white string tie and a conservative skirt or slacks. Anyone dumb enough to vary from that requirement would immediately get a scolding from the Court. An adjournment would be called and the offending lawyer told to change into appropriate clothing before returning to Court.

Do you think this type of behaviour might negatively impact the lawyer's case? Do you think this is a ridiculous example that would never happen in the real world? Think again. It has, and it does. The Court, rightfully so, demands respect, not only in dress but in how lawyers interact with other lawyers and how they deal with rulings of the Court with which they disagree. There is a strict formality to the process that must be followed to maintain the integrity of the administration of justice, like it or not.

In the day-to-day practice, firms adopted what they called "Casual Fridays." However, what was "casual" to one was "grubby and disheveled" to another. People, being people, would push the envelope as far as they could. Blue jeans, sweatshirts, no socks—you get the picture. One did not have to be all that sharp to figure out what would happen with these "casual" days, and I refused to allow Casual Fridays to occur in my firm. Clients expected lawyers to look professional, and I was not about to disappoint them. Our offices were first class, and I wanted our lawyers to not only be good at what they did but look like lawyers while they did it. On the other hand, if lawyers wanted to work evenings and weekends, I couldn't care less what they wore.

Another area that I felt strongly about was the appearance of our lawyers when they were in public, for example, traveling in an aircraft on personal or firm business. Our lawyers were, first and foremost, representatives of the firm. I wanted them to be an extension of our firm's image even when on personal time. I didn't want a good client to bump into one of our lawyers who looked like a slob while at an airport or elsewhere. Harsh, I know, and probably frowned upon now, but that is the way I did things then and the way I would do things now. If you want to go to work looking unkempt and slovenly, why not try another line of work?

My Advice: Remember what I said earlier? The hardest part of the practice of law is getting

*the work in the door. Most clients expect their
lawyers to look the part, so why in the world
would you greet a client looking like a bum and
take the chance of losing that client's business?*

▸ **Inflated company expense accounts must
be dealt with.**

When it came to expense account claims, a partner
of mine at Mason & Company used to say that
seventy-five percent were legitimate, ten percent
were shaky, and fifteen percent were out-and-out
fraud. He was correct. Expense accounts speak
volumes about an individual's veracity. I seldom
questioned expense accounts; notwithstanding,
expenses were not paid until they were reviewed
and approved by me. If a hard-working lawyer
wanted to take his wife and some "pretend clients"
for dinner, I would turn a blind eye. However,
when I witnessed a large number of golfers sitting
on the patio at the Willow Park Golf and Country
Club, drinking with their pals (few if any being
clients of the firm and those that were, were my
clients), and then seeing an expense account submitted for the drinks, I would say something in
a tone that had the intended result. Another act
that caused me grief and spoke to the honesty of

one particular lawyer occurred when this partner submitted an expense account for a dinner that had taken place while he was on vacation in the Okanagan. Acting like a big shot, he had picked up the tab for dinner for him and his wife's friends, who were not clients of the firm.

> **My Advice:** *Monitor expense accounts. If you see abuses, keep an eye on the situation, and make an issue of unjustifiable expenses only if a lawyer becomes a serious problem in this regard.*

▸ *The partnership agreement must reflect the best interests of the firm.*

Decisions that affect the law firm must always be made with the best interests of the firm in mind. Too many managers make decisions based on how they might be affected personally.

For example, I insisted that our Partnership Agreement contain language that required a partner leaving the firm to forfeit their capital should they compete against the firm within two years of their departure. This was harsh. However, it affected me more than any other partner at the time the agreements were signed. As previously noted, I wanted lawyers to specialize, and

I wanted the free flow of files within the office so the lawyer best suited to handle a client's problem would do so. I wanted to alleviate the worry of passing a file—and practically speaking, the client—to another partner and then having that partner leave the firm and take the client with them. Partners could leave the firm, but there was a cost associated with doing so.

The other reason for that clause in the Partnership Agreement was to make it more difficult for a partner to leave. Arguments arise from time to time, and sometimes those arguments are intense and even physical. I did not want to make it easy for a partner, in a huff, to announce their departure. The partner was welcome to go, but my expectation was that the Partnership Agreement would be honoured and done so for the best interests of the firm.

That said, we did have one partner who was a real problem. One day I received a call from a senior member of the Court of Queen's Bench. He started the conversation by advising that our firm had a problem. He went on to explain that this partner of the firm was rude and overly confrontational to other lawyers and the Court. His behaviour was having a negative impact on how our firm was being perceived by the judiciary. Obviously, I was upset over what I was being told. However, I thought I would double-check by contacting my former principal, Justice Blair Mason, to see if he had noticed the same problems with this guy. To my disappointment, he confirmed what the other Justice had said and offered to meet with this partner of mine to see if he could do some behaviour modification. The partner agreed to meet with Justice Mason. For a time his behaviour changed for the better, but, I am told, it did not last.

After we had words, this fellow finally left. He then tried to get around the Partnership Agreement by ostensibly joining a firm well outside the geographic prohibition contained in our agreement when, in fact, he was practicing well within the prohibited area. I really didn't care that this fellow would be competing against us, as he was not a person who generated business. In addition, his abrasive attitude to virtually everyone had reflected badly on our firm and gotten him into trouble with the judiciary.

I was not sorry to see this fellow go. Not only did he cheat by not living up to the provisions of our Partnership Agreement, but he had the gall to write to many of our firm's clients asking for them to follow him. Few, if any, took him up on his offer. Even though I was glad to see the tail end of this guy, I was disappointed that he turned out to be such a classless individual. This was especially upsetting since I had given him a job when he had been fired by another firm. I thought he might change. He did not. His departure was in the best interests of the firm.

> ***My Advice:*** *Include a clause in the Partnership Agreement that requires a partner leaving the firm to not compete against the firm within a defined geographical area for a reasonable period of time after the partner's departure or forfeit their capital. This is in the best interest of the firm.*

▸ Sabbaticals are not always in the best interests of the firm.

While I was practicing law, some law firms decided to implement a sabbatical policy for partners of their firms. Initially the idea was that lawyers could spend the extra time advancing their area of expertise by taking continuing education courses or doing something that would make them better and more productive members of their firm. This idea was quickly replaced with trips to Europe and other vacation destinations. The duration of sabbaticals varied, but I believe on average they were three months.

The lawyer on sabbatical would be paid by the firm for three months while the lawyer "recharged his or her batteries." Practically speaking, the effective down time was much longer. To go away for three months from a busy practice required at least two months to get ready to leave and another two months to get back up to speed upon returning from sabbatical. And while all of this is going on, a different lawyer had to get familiarized with a client's file. It was presumed that the client would relate to the replacement lawyer and would not be billed for the time it took to familiarize the replacement lawyer with the client's file.

I never liked the sabbatical concept, as I thought it was counterproductive to my desire to build a successful law firm. As a result, there were no sabbaticals during my reign. Of course, that policy was changed by my successors. By that time, the firm was more established; Calgary had enjoyed economic prosperity, and the economy had experienced twenty years of continual growth. It was pretty hard not to be successful as a law firm or, for that matter, any other business.

Within the last few years, things have become more difficult. Oil prices, upon which Calgary's economy is based, fell from more than one hundred dollars a barrel to the mid-thirties. Small- to medium-sized oil and gas companies were hit hard; many did not survive the reduction in revenue as they were unable to service the debt they had accumulated despite the historically low interest rates. In this economic environment, it will be interesting to see if the sabbatical idea survives. I do not think it will, nor do I think it should.

My Advice: Consider your policy regarding sabbaticals in light of current economic conditions. In reality, three-month sabbaticals affect the productivity of a firm for at least seven months. As a result, sabbaticals are not always in the best interests of the firm.

RULE #3

Promptly send out a reasonable bill

▶ A successful firm pays attention to billing their files on a consistent and regular basis. The accounts must be sent promptly after the work is complete or has reached an appropriate stage to justify sending an account. Accounts must clearly itemize the work that was done but, most importantly, reflect clear value for the services provided.

Had I been an independently wealthy man who did not require an income, I would have done legal work for nothing and thus avoided what I found to be the most difficult aspect of the practice.

However, I was not independently wealthy, and my employees depended on me and my partners to run a successful legal business, and that entailed charging a fee for the legal services we provided.

Invoices sent to clients had to be fair and reasonable if you wanted to keep the invoice's recipient as a client. Generally speaking, lawyers charge in six-minute increments or .1 hours. In fact, six minutes is the smallest unit of time for keeping time records. Accordingly, if a lawyer gets a twenty-second telephone call, most lawyers will bill for six minutes. An email arrives: six minutes, and so on. And lawyers say they don't pad their time!

I knew if I did that type of thing, the clients I had cultivated would quickly drop me as their lawyer. My clients knew what legal services were worth, and if you tried to "six minute" them to death, they would find another lawyer. It absolutely amazes me that many lawyers do not understand that concept. Big firms with large clients tend to get away with billing a client for every move on a file because the big corporate guy approving the big law firm's account does not, as they say, have "any skin in the game." That is, it's not his money! The vast majority of my clients were spending their own funds. As a result, they scrutinized our accounts carefully. If clients perceived us as being unfair, they would simply find another lawyer.

That is why it is so important to send out a bill that is not only fair and reasonable but is perceived as such by your client.

8

A FAIR ACCOUNTING

VIRTUALLY EVERY client with a legal problem wants their problem solved as quickly as possible and for a fair price. The most common way of arriving at an end price or a total of fees owing is to keep track of the time a lawyer spends on solving a client's problem. Time is used as a guide, but lawyers are allowed by The Rules of Court, in virtually all jurisdictions in Canada, to bonus their time for things like complexity, urgency, the result obtained and the lawyer's expertise in a particular area. However, the basic yardstick is time spent, and time is what a lawyer is selling.

When a client receives a bill from a lawyer, the subject matter of the account cannot be held, lived in, driven, watched or admired. We sell only our time, and time is intangible. Time is a much harder sell than a new car, a painting or a new TV to name but a few things that can give the perception of value. For this reason, lawyers and clients often clash when a client gets a huge, unanticipated bill. In cases like this, it is usually the lawyer who is at fault for not keeping the client informed of the accumulating costs. Too many lawyers are hesitant to "talk money" with their clients. Usually a well-informed client will not complain about an account as long as it is perceived as being fair for the amount of work that was required to solve the problem. In effect, a client must be satisfied that there is value received for the money being charged. What causes problems is a surprise bill that in the client's mind bears no relationship to the problem being solved. And rest assured, there are too many lawyers who charge what they think the "traffic will bear." Those lawyers run the very real risk of losing their client(s) to a competitor who charges a fair fee and who does not take advantage of clients.

> ### *A "fair accounting" means an accurate record of billable hours.*

We started doing a reasonable amount of personal injury litigation, sometimes referred to as "ambulance chasing." Payment for this type of litigation was based on contingency fees, which were a percentage of the amount recovered by the client. The client was not required to pay anything unless the firm was successful in collecting money for the client. The firm paid all disbursements up front, which were recovered when the file was settled.

While this system was banned in some jurisdictions for many years, it was an acceptable practice in the Province of Alberta. The usual fee charged was approximately thirty percent of the amount recovered plus disbursements incurred (which were usually paid by the insurance company) and taxable costs. This was a very lucrative area of the practice, but it required a huge cash flow to be generated from other areas of the practice in order to carry the accumulative disbursement costs for a large number of personal injury files.

Enter the solicitor area of the practice, which financed the costs of running a personal injury file inventory.

I was never totally confident that we were making money on these files. I recognized that cash was coming in from the various settlements, but I wanted to know how the time spent on these files translated into fees. That is, were we making money, or weren't we? To satisfy my concerns in this regard, I wanted accurate time recorded on all personal injury files. Doing so made complete sense to me but, of course, there were lawyers who didn't want to do what I wanted done. When I insisted that they comply, they reluctantly did so.

I put them in a box because litigation lawyers liked to brag about how many billable hours they had amassed in a year. However, if they "gilded the billable-hour lily" too much, their files would show a loss on a time-incurred basis; the hourly return went down, and they would have me to deal with.

One time I had a lawyer who billed in excess of seventy hours on various files while on a two-week holiday in Kelowna. When I quizzed him on how that was possible, I discovered that while he was away, his secretary had opened new files and had sent out standard letters and then entered a fixed amount of time on the billing sheet for what had been done. Of course, she had followed her boss's less-than-honourable instructions.

This particular lawyer (and some others) was constantly trying to game the systems I had put in place for the benefit of the firm. This fellow would, seemingly, spend hours trying to get around our systems in an effort to enhance his reputation within the firm. Unfortunately, he didn't fool anyone, and as a result of his antics over the years, he lost credibility amongst virtually all members of the firm.

> *My Advice:* Be alert for lawyers who are "gaming the system" and not providing an accurate accounting of their billable hours.

▸ **Waiting too long to bill a client can have several unpleasant ramifications.**

It was my experience that far too many lawyers needed to be coaxed and prodded every month to prepare and send out accounts on files that were completed or where an interim account was appropriate. Virtually every month, as we approached month end, I would have to send a memo to all lawyers reminding them that the end of the month was fast approaching and that it was time for them to address their minds to billing their clients.

Although this may be bewildering to a businessperson, lawyers were notorious for avoiding the task of sending out timely invoices. Some, if anyone can believe it, would want to bill their files only a few times a year even though the services provided had concluded months before. This delay tactic was a recipe for economic disaster for any business. Imagine a car dealer or an appliance store not collecting payment for the car or the fridge for six or eight months after the sale was made. Or giving the car or fridge to a customer and not invoicing for either for months. No businessperson with a brain in their head would do that, and a lawyer who delays sending an invoice is, to say the least, lacking in business acumen.

Not only were accounts slow to go out to clients, but substantial out-of-pocket expenses were incurred by the firm on behalf of clients. These expenses are called disbursements, and believe me, they can add up. Several years ago the managing partner of my old firm told me that, on personal injury files alone, the combined disbursements were approaching six million dollars. So, the lawyer who neglected sending timely accounts to clients could really cause a firm economic grief in more ways than one.

As far as my personal practice was concerned, as soon as a file was completed or had reached a stage to justify a bill being sent, out it went. In fact, every month, I looked at every one of my files to see if it was appropriate to send an account. It was pretty obvious to me that sending and then collecting the invoice was fundamentally important to the survival and growth of our business. One would think that truism would be understood by everyone. Not so. I had to pester too many of our lawyers, on an ongoing basis, to get them to do the obvious.

Lawyers who delayed sending invoices were usually the same lawyers who had difficulty collecting funds owed to the firm and were often the lawyers who had disputes with their clients over the size of an account. So much time had passed since the work being billed for had been completed that the client lost track of what exactly it was the lawyer had done. The account, when received, became an unpleasant and upsetting surprise resulting in a strained relationship between lawyer and client.

My Advice: Usually clients will not complain about an account, provided the lawyer keeps

*the client informed of what is transpiring on
a file and sends out an account as close to the
completion of the work as possible and while
the services performed are still fresh in the
client's mind.*

▶ ***Send out an itemized account.***

To be fair to the client, an account must itemize
exactly what the lawyer did and when the work
was done. Some lawyers—lazy lawyers, usually—
think it is just fine to send an account that reads
simply: "For all professional services rendered
between the ____day of _____ 201– and the
____day of _____ 201–, OUR FEE _____."

Just think for a moment how you would feel
receiving such an invoice. It doesn't tell you anything about what the person actually did in return
for the fee being demanded.

I can somewhat understand a lawyer pro-
crastinating over preparing an itemized account,
especially if the lawyer has not kept proper track
of the time spent on behalf of a client. If a lawyer
does keep accurate time records and itemizes
what has been done for the client, preparing a
final account is not a chore and could, in fact, be

easily done by the lawyer's secretary using the properly completed time sheets.

My Advice: Today, any well-run law firm will require (or demand) time slips or computer time inputs to be submitted at the end of each day. If time spent on files is not recorded and submitted as mandated, the firm's accounting department will be in immediate contact with the tardy lawyer, looking for an explanation. If law firms today seem to resemble a nineteenth-century sweatshop, where every minute of every day must be accounted for, perhaps you can understand why lawyers pad their time. If they do not perform, especially in large firms, their futures will not be very bright.

Caveat Emptor applies when hiring legal representation...

I had a close friend and client who decided to sell his very successful business to one of his employees and entered into negotiations with the employee. By this time, I had retired from the practice, but my friend continued to seek my advice. While negotiations with the employee proceeded, my friend asked me who at my old firm he should use to paper the transaction. I suggested he use a senior corporate commercial lawyer I had hired many years before and who I knew would do a really good job for my friend.

I called the lawyer and told him what was going on and asked if he would do the legal work. He apologized and told me that he was so busy he simply did not have time to do the work but suggested another lawyer in the firm be retained. The problem I had at this point was that I knew the lawyer who was recommended. I had an uneasy feeling about his ability to do this particular task, but I was assured he could do the job.

He was retained by my friend. The draft agreement that was ultimately produced by this guy did not at all reflect the terms of the transaction. It was, in fact, gibberish. I then took it upon myself to start redrafting the offending clauses, and while this was going on, two things happened: my friend got seriously ill and almost died, and his lawyer went on holidays. The vacationing lawyer left the file with a guy I had hired on the recommendation of a good friend who was a prominent member of a very large, highly regarded Calgary law firm. My friend had, at one point, been a mentor to this guy while he was a student in the combined MBA/LLB program at the University of Calgary.

Anyway, this lad took over the file, and things went from bad to worse. He seemed to have great difficulty understanding the terms of the deal and continued to send me drafts of the proposed agreement that, simply stated, did not even come close to reflecting the terms of the transaction agreed to by the parties. After many late nights spent redrafting agreement after agreement, I suggested to my friend that we fire my old firm, and he agreed.

Although I was retired, I was still a member of the Law Society of Alberta, so I called the lawyer for the purchaser, told him what had transpired, and informed him that he would, going forward, be dealing with me. We finalized the agreement in short order. Because I was retired, I no longer had a trust account or the infrastructure to, on a practical level, conclude the transaction. I contacted a lawyer who had previously been a partner in my firm and who had left to work for a client of the firm. He subsequently returned to the practice of law but with a firm other than ours. I knew this fellow, and I was more than confident that he could wrap up and finalize the deal for my friend.

He was retained, and the deal closed quickly, efficiently and for a fair fee. I considered the matter at an end until I received a call from my friend advising that the first lawyer at my old firm had sent him a bill for $38,000, as I recall.

I was livid to say the least! I phoned the lawyer in question and suggested that there must be some mistake. I was advised that there was no mistake; the fee charged was commensurate with the size of the transaction and would not be reduced. I saw red! I told this fellow that had I still been the managing partner of the firm and he had submitted the work to me that he submitted to my friend, he would have been out of a job. I also told him that my friend was not going to pay his account and that we would have it taxed by the Clerk of the Court. A client can take advantage of this process if a lawyer's account is disputed. The Clerk of the Court has the power to maintain or reduce the account. I told him that the former founder and senior partner of his firm would give evidence as to the quality of his work. I had the numerous drafts of the agreement to support my position that his account was ridiculously excessive under the circumstances. After some posturing and my successor at the firm getting involved, the account was dramatically reduced.

The lawyer who sent the account and his colleague are examples of lawyers I should have fired and didn't. In my heart I knew that these guys were not, under any definition, good lawyers. The funny thing is, the more senior guy had a reputation as a "rainmaker," being someone who could attract business to the firm—a scary situation to be sure.

RULE #4

Make sure you collect your bills
(and watch where the money goes!)

▶ Once you get the work in the door, complete the required tasks, and send your client a fair account, your work is still not complete. Now you must ensure that the account is paid and paid as quickly as possible. Ignoring this final Rule can be devastating for your firm's economic viability. You can do everything I suggest to make your firm successful, but if you do not pay attention to something as fundamental as getting paid, everything else is irrelevant.

For God's sake, make sure you get paid!

9

MAKING SURE
YOU GET PAID

As surprising as this may sound, the average lawyer, unless held to account by a managing partner, does not pay attention to collecting accounts receivable. In fact, most lawyers are awful businesspeople, lacking the most basic understanding of how to run a successful business. Something as fundamental as collecting their accounts receivable in a timely fashion is a concept beyond the vast majority of lawyers. However, ignoring this most basic and fundamental Rule is a recipe for disaster.

One way to avoid the unpleasantness of chasing your clients to pay outstanding accounts is to demand a retainer in advance of starting the legal work. Many clients expect to pay a retainer but, of course, will not do so unless asked. In fact, most clients have a good feeling about buying a lawyer's expertise when they pay a retainer. And it is a very good idea to keep the retainer topped up as your legal work continues.

Without a retainer, the issue of collecting accounts receivable is an ongoing, time-consuming yet essential element of running a successful law firm.

▸ *Hold accounts receivable meetings to motivate lawyers to collect outstanding accounts.*

On the first Monday of every month, I would convene an accounts receivable meeting. These meetings involved all lawyers in the firm and were a command performance. Just about everyone, excluding me, hated these meetings. Starting at 7:30 a.m., the meetings lasted a couple of hours. Once a lawyer's accounts receivable were discussed, that lawyer could leave the meeting and go back to work.

Collection of accounts receivable was an ongoing problem. As the end of the month neared, I would have to remind everyone to get their accounts in and then keep after the lawyers to collect what they had billed. One would think that both these requirements were pretty basic, but left to their own devices, lawyers billed files late—if at all—and outstanding accounts may or may not get collected. That was not going to happen on my watch, and I was not quiet about what I expected of the lawyers in our firm when it came to those two basic requirements.

However, even though I ranted, raved, threatened and cajoled, there were still some incorrigible souls who just never understood the importance of billing on a timely basis and then taking the necessary steps to collect what they had billed.

The infamous accounts receivable meetings turned out to be a necessity for the economic well-being of our firm. The meetings worked like this: prior to the meeting, every lawyer in the firm was given a list of their accounts receivable. We met in our largest boardroom. The room became quite crowded as the firm grew, and we rolled in extra chairs to accommodate everyone. Based on the schedules of various lawyers, we started the process, lawyer by lawyer, concentrating on accounts over sixty days—and especially those over ninety days. I asked the lawyer involved the reason as to why the client had not paid their bill and whether or not the lawyer had called the client.

As you can imagine, I got varying responses (excuses) such as, "Fred says he plans to pay the account when his brother-in-law, who owes him money, sells his cottage." I had Mark Rathwell, a young litigator whom I really liked, sit beside me during the meeting; I would tell the lawyer who just explained why "Fred" had not paid his account that I did not give a "rat's ass" (actually, I used much stronger language) about Fred's brother-in-law or his cottage. I explained the obvious: I had absolutely no interest in what was going on between Fred and his brother-in-law. I would advise the lawyer to call Fred and let him know that I wanted the account paid by the end of that week. The lawyer could make me out to be the bad guy if that helped. I would then say to Mark Rathwell, "If by Friday you do not hear from me that this account is paid or that satisfactory arrangements have been made to pay the account, I want you to issue a Statement of

Claim on Monday." Sometimes the lawyer would argue that we couldn't do that because Fred was a good client of the firm. My response was that, unlike Fred, "good clients" paid their bills in a timely fashion. If not dealt with, so-called "good clients" like Fred could cause our firm serious grief or worse.

I continued this process around the table, and as each lawyer had a turn, they would leave the meeting. You would be amazed how these meetings caused accounts to be paid and the money to roll in. In fact, as time went by, the mere delivery of a memo reminding everyone of an upcoming accounts receivable meeting would result in telephone calls to clients and, in many cases, old accounts paid. The lawyers involved did not want to go through my interrogation; they preferred to be in a position to announce that an old account had been paid.

The idea that I had to go to such measures to collect accounts was disconcerting, but left alone our lawyers and their "good clients" would have caused the firm serious financial difficulty. As a result of these meetings (and of keeping on top of accounts receivable in general), we wrote off very few accounts.

I was not immune to the above process. As previously noted, I referred many clients whom I had introduced to the firm to other lawyers in the office whose legal expertise was better suited to do the work required by the client. Sometimes these clients were too slow in paying their accounts, and their tardiness would come up at our accounts receivable meetings. The lawyer who had done the work and sent the bill would remind me that the culprit was one of my referrals. Of course, the lawyer was correct, so I would take it upon myself to follow up with the client.

> *My Advice: While accounts receivable meetings are not popular, they result in accounts getting paid and money coming in.*

▶ **The decision to fire a client who did not pay his outstanding account was a difficult decision made in the best interests of the firm.**

I once had a client who was a reasonably large home builder. I had known the founder and president of the company from when we were in our early teens and both worked part-time at a grocery store. This guy was a born entrepreneur. Although involved in all kinds of businesses, home building was his main business as an adjunct to his professional employment. Eventually he abandoned everything except home building, and to this day he builds residential and assisted-living units all over North America.

Over the years, we became really good friends. We did all his and his company's legal work. However, this lad was not above suing people for various wrongs—real or perceived—and we would do his bidding (or, at least, I would have someone in our litigation department go after whoever happened to be the defendant *du jour*). Although this fellow did not mind paying a law firm a reasonable fee for conveying his homes to purchasers, he had an affinity for delaying the payment of litigation accounts.

During one of the accounts receivable meetings, one or more of the litigation lawyers who did work for this guy pointed out that my friend's outstanding accounts were really my problem. They were right. After the meeting I phoned my friend and told him that his inattention to these litigation accounts had become an embarrassment to me; his delay in paying made it really difficult for me to put pressure on other members of the firm to collect their accounts receivable and, as a result, were causing me practical grief. His reply was, "I do not want to talk about this!" I said, "We have to talk about it." He repeated his position: he just didn't want to talk about the matter.

Obviously, his response was unacceptable and upsetting. We had followed his instructions, and we had done the work required. We were not always successful in these litigious matters, and we did not always get the result he wanted. We were not working for him on a contingency basis, so win, lose or draw, we expected to be paid. I stewed about this matter for several days, talked to some of my partners, and came to the conclusion that, in the best interest of our firm, I would have to fire this client.

I phoned my client and asked if he had any free time to see me. He acted as if nothing was amiss and suggested we meet at his office at four o'clock that afternoon. I showed up at the appointed time, and we sat down in his office. I started the conversation by reminding him that we had known one another for thirty years and that he had been a good client of our firm as it grew in size. For those reasons, I felt I owed it to him to tell him face-to-face that we were no longer prepared to do his legal work. I asked him to take all reasonable steps to move his legal work to another law firm.

You know, I got the impression that he could have been knocked over by a feather. He seemed genuinely shocked that I would ask him and his businesses to leave our firm. However, I felt I had no choice. Every decision I made as the managing partner of our firm was a decision made not necessarily in my personal best interest but in the best interest of the entity known as McLeod & Company. Our firm would have been even more successful than it already was if others in the firm had taken the same approach.

My former client continues to be extremely successful, and by making the point I felt I had to make, our firm left a lot of money on the table. Today, my former client/friend and I are cordial to one another when our paths cross, but the close friendship that once existed is, sadly, over.

> *My Advice: Tackle difficult topics head-on, whether it's with clients or members of the firm. Remember that hard decisions, even those that affect you personally, must be made in the best interest of the firm.*

10

MANAGING THE FIRM'S FINANCES

IN MY EXPERIENCE, few law firms pay enough attention to managing their firm's finances. By not paying attention to the business of the practice of law, they end up needing to do really dumb things like financing accounts receivable and, in some instances—if you can believe it—work in progress! These firms borrow too much money to pay for partners' draws, the salaries for associates, secretarial and support staff, and general office overhead.

It would seem obvious that managing the finances is fundamental to maintaining and perpetuating a successful firm. However, you would be surprised at what masquerades as good business management within too many law firms. Over the past decade, lawyers and law firms have been extremely busy, and this activity has masked a large number of really bad business decisions. If the economy tightens, as history suggests it surely will, ignoring the proper management of a firm's finances will have devastating results for many firms. In fact, I heard a rumour recently that the partners of a prominent Calgary oil and gas firm got a cash call to keep the firm operational. The protracted low oil prices can badly hurt a firm that does not react to changing economic circumstances quickly enough.

▶ *Keep borrowing to a minimum.*

I was adamantly opposed to borrowing money from banks unless it was absolutely necessary. I did not want a banker as my partner, sitting in our partners meetings dictating to us what we could or could not do and what equipment we could or could not buy. By not owing money, we were free to run the firm as we (I) saw fit and do so without the interference of some banker.

Besides that, in my experience bankers fall all over themselves to give you money when you don't need it. I would use the analogy that a banker would be happy to lend you an umbrella when the sun was shining, but with the slightest drop of rain, they would take the umbrella back. Simply stated: I didn't trust them. When negotiating a loan, the bank would often assure us that the interest rate would be the prime lending rate plus one half percent. They would then "check with their head office in Toronto" and many times would come back saying they were "allowed" by their head office to authorize only prime plus *one* percent. As we really didn't absolutely need the money, I would tell them, "Thanks, but we'll pass." In all cases they would come back and advise that Toronto had reconsidered.

My Advice: Borrow for such things as leasehold improvements and large capital expenses, but make sure the loans are paid down rapidly.

Early finances...

As a youngster, besides working hard and long, I made money. Although I started out at 82 cents per hour, I always had money to save and spend.

At my father's urging, I started depositing money with Investors Syndicate. When I graduated from law school and was an articling student, I had enough money saved for a down payment on the first house my wife Brenda and I bought. It was an up-down duplex, and we rented out the lower level to a young family. I made $375.00 per month as an articling student, and our mortgage payment was $185.00, so the $75.00 per month we received in rent helped a great deal.

▶ *Build up your firm's capital accounts.*

By keeping our borrowing to a minimum, we were able to build up our respective capital accounts within the firm. As previously noted, we defined "capital" as a combination of cash in the bank, incurred but unbilled disbursements, accounts receivable under ninety days, furniture at depreciated value and work in progress—minus debt. Goodwill was not factored into the equation because it was my feeling that once a lawyer was offered a partnership, they had already contributed to the goodwill of the firm.

We used the value of the capital account for new partners buying into the firm. It was a fair and easily justifiable number. When a partner retired but did not compete with the firm, the partner was paid out his accumulated capital quarterly over three years with the prime rate of interest charged on the decreasing balance. I was owed a large sum of money when I retired, and the firm paid me in full and on time.

My Advice: Building up and maintaining capital accounts is good business practice and also builds long-term value for partners in the firm.

FINAL THOUGHTS

11

THE VALUE OF JOINING
VARIOUS ASSOCIATIONS

I FELT THIS BOOK would not be complete without a few thoughts on the value of joining various associations, as these bodies can absorb much of a lawyer's time and money. As there is not a "Rule" to cover this, I thought it best to include it in my final thoughts to you.

As a lawyer practicing in the Canadian provincial and territorial jurisdictions, one can get involved with various legal-related associations. However, I really do not think that belonging to the local Bar Association or the Canadian Bar

Association (CBA) contributes to the success of a law firm. Such memberships may enhance relationships with other lawyers in your community. But, as far as contributing to the success of a law firm, they are, for all intents and purposes, a waste of time and money. With the exception of educational initiatives undertaken by Canadian Bar Association volunteers at the local levels, the CBA does nothing, in my view, to contribute to the success of a law firm.

Provincial law societies in Canada are a command performance. Lawyers practicing in every jurisdiction must belong to their provincial or territorial law society. Each law society is governed by a board of directors made up of lawyers practicing in that jurisdiction, who are called "Benchers." Benchers are elected every two years by the lawyers practicing in each jurisdiction.

▸ *The Canadian Bar Association*

With the exception of various sections of the Canadian Bar Association (CBA) and their educational programs, in my opinion the CBA is a left-wing advocacy group that clearly does not represent entrepreneurial members of the profession. If you like to party and get your picture in the CBA newsletter, or should you aspire to be a judge someday, then by all means, get involved. By working your way up within your provincial branch and perhaps someday becoming a member of the executive, you will have taken the first step in enhancing your resume for possible appointment to the provincial or federal bench. If that is your goal, then by all means, join up.

Belonging to the CBA is not cheap. You will have to decide if the benefits are worth the cost. The total cost of belonging to the CBA is very high for a large firm, and I just couldn't find the value in being a member. The CBA did not represent my views, and its mission continued to remind me of the ultra-left-wing folks I had attended law school with at Osgoode Hall.

Most lawyers want to be members of the CBA simply because they believe that is what they should do. Perhaps, as an added benefit, their firm might spring for a trip to whatever city the CBA picks for its annual meeting, giving lawyers the opportunity to attend more dinners and parties. Of course, there will be various seminars, most exceedingly boring, with representative speakers from various levels of our Courts and political persuasions (almost always liberals), and business leaders and lawyers said to be prominent in their fields of expertise.

During my days as a practicing lawyer, I was asked to chair some CBA panels involving new developments in the law of real property. Instead of letting me find the best lawyers to join me on my panel, I was instructed to have representation from northern, central and southern Alberta. Also, it was made clear to me that including a woman on the panel would be a good idea. I always found these directions odd; I just assumed they would want me to assemble the best and most knowledgeable lawyers on my panel, regardless of their gender or where they practiced law.

> ***My Advice:*** *Join the CBA if you must, but I can guarantee you that there are better ways to spend your firm's money. What I did as a compromise was to allow one lawyer from each department of our firm to join the CBA. The lawyer who attended the section meetings would then send a memo to all members of the firm if anything of interest to our firm was brought up during the section meeting. This compromise made sense to me and seemed to work quite well.*

Bucking the system...

Not only did I not like Osgoode as part of York University, but I couldn't wait to get out of there and away from its culture.

Gerald Le Dain was the dean of the law school, but he was busy chairing the Le Dain Commission on Drug Abuse in Canada. Some students were hired by various professors to do one thing or another. These students were paid, given offices, and received course credits from the professor who hired them. Some of these students did work on Le Dain's Commission.

I wrote articles in the law school newspaper "Obiter Dicta," under the pen name Gamble Benedict. I was afraid to use my real name, but some people figured it out, I think. The gist of my articles was to reveal the unfairness of what was going on at the school regarding some students being treated more preferentially than others. For those who were interested, I also provided a guideline for getting through Osgoode with high grades without working very hard. I even pointed out the professors to follow from subject to subject. Actually going to law school to learn something substantive about the law of the land was not, it seemed, a priority for some of the classmates.

My revelations caused quite a stir within the law school. The dean and others attempted to dispute my allegations during some large meetings. To their credit, the editors of the "Obiter Dicta" never revealed who Gamble Benedict was.

▸ *The Legal Education Society of Alberta*

The Legal Education Society of Alberta (LESA) is an offshoot of the Law Society of Alberta and, in theory, provides continuing education to members of the profession. LESA holds seminars on varying topics. Law Society members who purport to have special knowledge of certain areas of the law were recruited to lead these seminars. I was a panelist and occasionally chaired various panels.

I found those who ran LESA to be very bureaucratic in their approach to fulfilling their mandate. When LESA could have provided leadership on contentious issues within various areas of practice, they refused to get involved. Too many times they left problems festering amongst members of the law society.

Today, unlike when I practiced, lawyers are required to attend a certain number of LESA-sponsored, continuing legal education seminars.

While this is a good thing in theory, I could never shake the suspicion that this continuing-education requirement was put in place to justify the survival of a mediocre organization.

> *My Advice: The seminars offered by LESA are not cheap, and in too many instances, lawyers leave the seminars thinking that they were of limited value and not worth the time spent. Pick your seminars wisely.*

▶ *The Law Society of Alberta*

As every lawyer reading this book knows, the Law Society of Alberta is the organization that governs the lawyers within the province, and it does so in accordance with the provisions of the Legal Professions Act. The Law Society's day-to-day functions are handled by an Executive Director of the Law Society, along with a large number of people who do various jobs, supposedly for the benefit of the lawyers practicing law in the province.

A group of lawyers, referred to as the Benchers of the Law Society, is elected by lawyers in the province. These folks act as chair or vice-chair of various committees. Other members of these committees are appointed by the Benchers from the ranks of the Law Society members. The wide range of committees includes a Conduct Committee. The Conduct Committee investigates misconduct and can charge a member with various offences that constitute conduct unbecoming a Barrister and Solicitor. In addition, the committee can refer a matter involving a wayward lawyer to a hearing panel made up of three Benchers. There also exists an Education, Professional Responsibility, Audit, Insurance, Practice Review, Land Titles Liaison Committee and others.

I just about forgot; there are also several so-called "lay" or nonlawyer Benchers who, in my experience, are usually political appointees or friends of the powers that be within the Law Society. Some of these lay Benchers are very good, but as in life in general, some not so much.

For a volunteer position, Benchers have a very heavy workload. Generally speaking, they do a good job. Each month there is a Benchers Meeting, the location of which alternates between Calgary and Edmonton. Several days before each meeting, the Benchers are provided with binders full of background information pertaining to various subjects on the meeting agenda. Those who take the time to review the content of the binders—and not all do—find it to be a daunting and time-intensive task. I know all of this because I was appointed a Bencher and acted in that capacity for two years.

Being a Bencher and having a say in how the Practice of Law was governed in the province was important to me. Within my area of the day-to-day practice, there were problematic issues that cried out to be rectified. However, most Benchers are elected as a result of their names being recognized as prominent litigation lawyers, both criminal and civil. Or, they may belong to large firms and, if there is a form of voting reciprocity, get members of other large firms to support them. Those lawyers who went to law school in Alberta know many lawyers who went to school with them. Then there were the lady lawyers who, many speculated, tended to support lady candidates. Women quickly became a dominant force within the Law Society and expressed a preference to making the Law Society of Alberta a "kinder and gentler place." I shall leave it to others to debate whether lawyers in Alberta are better off today than they were in days gone by.

My Advice: I encourage any lawyer to get involved in the profession's governance. However, if you do, it would be best if your tolerance for frustration is high. It is a thankless job but is a stepping stone to a position on a Court, if that happens to be a job you may someday seek.

One story about the Law Society...

I would like to relate a story about an incident I once had with the Law Society of Alberta. A small law firm in Calgary interpreted a decision of the Alberta Court of Appeal to rule that it was no longer necessary for the law firm representing a homebuilder to hold back fifteen percent (it is now ten percent) of the cost of a new home, not including land value, for forty-five days following the substantial completion of the home, in compliance with the provisions of the Alberta Builders Lien Act. This firm proceeded to solicit legal work from builders by telling the builders that the firm would do their work and not hold back the fifteen percent. Of course, the idea of freeing up fifteen percent of their cash flow forty-five days earlier than before was appealing and well received by the builders.

Most lawyers disagreed with this small firm's interpretation of the Court of Appeal decision. Thoughtful lawyers believed that the actions of the small firm put all lawyers in Alberta at risk should a builder go bankrupt without the builder's lawyer maintaining the holdback mandated by the Builders Lien Act. The Act gave new-home purchasers protection; if the builder did not pay his trades or went bankrupt, the unpaid trades could place a lien on the title to the purchaser's new home. Provided the Builders Lien holdback of fifteen percent was maintained, the aggrieved homeowner would simply cause the lien holdback funds to be paid into Court, and the liens, regardless of their combined monetary value, would be removed from the title. The small firm was arguing that, in effect, the Builders Lien Act, at least as it pertained to holdbacks, had been gutted by the aforesaid Court of Appeal decision.

I, along with prominent lawyers in the area of real property law, brought this matter to the attention of the Law Society, thinking the Law Society would not be pleased with the risk it was assuming by allowing this small firm (and now others as well) to refuse to comply with Provincial Government legislation. To our complete surprise, and for reasons I still cannot comprehend, the Law Society did absolutely nothing and, instead, allowed this practice to continue. Fortunately for the Law Society, Alberta has enjoyed economic prosperity since this incident, and unless a builder was a total buffoon, making money selling new homes was a no-brainer. Few if any builders went bankrupt, leaving purchasers with liens on their titles. For all I know, bankrupt builders and liened titles may have occurred, and the Law Society quietly paid off the liens out of general or insurance funds.

In the midst of this Builders Lien debate, one of our secretaries bought a home from a builder represented by the small firm noted above. The builder refused to hold back under the Builders Lien Act and denied the purchaser possession of her new home if she insisted on a holdback being maintained. I saw this as an opportunity to have the matter clarified, so we sought an Order from the Court of Queen's Bench granting our client possession of her new home and also ordering that the fifteen percent holdback be maintained for the statutory period of time. We appeared before The Honourable Mr. Justice Montgomery (and those who knew the good Justice will understand when I say *that* was an experience unto itself), who granted our requests and gave me the orders I sought. By the way, the Law Society of

Alberta had intervened in the action because, of course, it wanted the matter resolved as well.

The builder appealed Justice Montgomery's decision to the Court of Appeal. On the day of the appeal, it became clear that the panel had not even read the Law Society's brief, and when made aware of its existence, they adjourned to read the document. To make a long story short, they refused to clarify the law, stating that the passage of time rendered the issue "moot." The three Court of Appeal judges came from the criminal and civil litigation end of the practice. They did not appear to understand what we were trying to get across. Even though we had been successful at the Court of Queen's Bench level, to rub salt in our wounds, they ordered us to pay costs to the builder in the sum of $25,000.

Alan Macleod was the president of the Law Society at the time (Al is now a Court of Queen's Bench Justice and a darn good one). He was absolutely livid with what the Court of Appeal panel had done. To his credit, Alan authorized the Law Society to pay half the costs, but we were on the hook for the other half. So much for trying to do what I still believe was the right thing. After this experience, I vowed to stop "tilting at windmills," as trying to get people to do the right thing was just too stressful (and expensive).

As a final aside, our firm lost several good builder clients as a result of this small firm's antics. On the bright side (for me anyway), I expanded my firm in other directions. We diversified away from builder's real estate conveyancing, although we still did work for builders who allowed us to comply with the law. I have been retired since 2004. However, the small firm is still small, and its members are still working away.

12

THE JUDICIAL SYSTEM

WHEN I WAS A YOUNG lawyer, there were four levels of Courts in the Province of Alberta, as well as in other provincial jurisdictions across Canada: the Supreme Court Appellant Division, the federal District Court, the federal Supreme Court Trial Division and the Provincial Small Claims Court, with a monetary claim limit of, I think, $2500.

The Federal Court Judges and Justices were appointed by the federal government and, obviously, the Province of Alberta appointed the Alberta Provincial Court Judges. These latter judges, besides hearing civil claims in Small Claims Court, also had a criminal section that dealt with comparatively minor criminal matters and Alberta Traffic Act violations.

The federal District Court generally heard matters of a less serious nature and acted as a Court of Appeal for cases decided by the Provincial Court. The District Court had a most useful function of getting civil disputes adjudicated very quickly. There was no discovery process. A Statement of Claim was filed and served on a defendant, and that person had a specified amount of time in which a Statement of Defence or Dispute Note had to be filed. The matter would then be placed on the District Court list to be spoken to, usually on a Friday afternoon, for trial dates to be set two weeks into the future. It was not unusual for a Statement of Claim to be filed and served on a defendant, a Statement of Defence filed, and a matter set down for trial all within two months. I recall the system working very well and litigants getting their various problems dealt with quickly, efficiently and affordably.

Then, sometime in the late 1970s or early '80s, the Canadian federal government, in its wisdom, decided to amalgamate the District Court and the Supreme Court of Alberta Trial Division into the Alberta Court of Queen's Bench Trial Division.

The Judges of the District Court were elevated *en masse* to Justices of the Court of Queen's Bench Trial Division.

Around that same time, the monetary limit of the Provincial Small Claims Court was increased to the princely sum of $5,000. The practical effect was that any monetary claim of more than $5,000 had to go to the Court of Queen's Bench and the more formal processes required by that Court. In my view, two things happened. First, the litigants were required to go through discoveries and other formalities designed for the more serious matters previously reserved for the attention of the Supreme Court of Alberta Trial Division. Second, the Justices of that Court were not particularly fond of spending their time dealing with minor matters that were previously dealt with by the District Court Judges.

Years passed, and inflation became a reality. The Alberta Provincial Court limit was recently raised to $50,000 (and in my opinion should be substantially higher). And, of course, the matters dealt with by the Court of Queen's Bench became more expensive and complex for the litigants.

I believe our judicial system has morphed into a system that neither works nor consistently provides justice to the citizens it is meant to serve. The delays in getting matters to trial are ridiculous, and in too many instances, the time it takes to get a judgement from the Court is scandalous. While all this is going on, legal fees have risen to the level where the average person cannot come close to being able to afford legal representation. A person may get justice and bankruptcy at the same time. I firmly believe that our judicial system works only for extremely wealthy individuals and corporations.

There is a saying I have heard about matrimonial lawyers; the saying is not funny to the litigants but is a perverse indictment of lawyers. It is: *When all the family money has been eaten up in legal fees, the lawyers agree on a settlement they recommend to their respective clients.* Although matrimonial lawyers will howl at this representation, just ask the people—including members of one of the Courts—who have endured accounts rendered by matrimonial lawyers, and I expect a great deal of support for my views on this subject.

During the past fifteen to twenty years, in an effort to avoid out-of-control legal fees, mediation/arbitration has become a popular alternative to taking a dispute to court. However, after

I retired, I participated as a member of several arbitration panels. I could not believe the fees that I was told I should charge by other panel members. What has occurred is that a fallback arbitration system has, over a relatively short period of time, developed into a system that rivals our courts as far as the end costs to the parties are concerned. As a result, the only practical effect is that litigants get hammered financially much faster via the mediation/arbitration route than they did by going through the morass known as our legal system.

The problem I had writing the foregoing is that I know many Court of Queen's Bench Justices, and I do not want to tar them all with the same brush. In fact, I suspect many of my friends who are current or past members of the Court will quietly agree with me. Recently I had occasion to discuss a case that has gone on far too long without the litigants getting a judgement of the Court, and I asked if the Chief Justice could not intervene and get some of the Justices he supervised to do their jobs in a more timely fashion. To my complete surprise, I was told that, once a Justice is appointed to the Court, there is nothing the Chief Justice can do to reprimand a Justice who is not doing his or her job in a timely fashion. Once appointed, accountability becomes a practical problem.

I admit that I do not attend the Court House in Calgary very frequently, but when I do attend, I've noticed that a large number of the courtrooms are empty. Yet delays are rampant. I am told that the fault lies with the federal government delaying the appointment of additional Justices. While I'm sure that has contributed to the delays, I get the feeling that the Court, generally speaking, lacks urgency. Time doesn't matter. If something gets resolved this month, that's fine, but if it doesn't, no big deal. The idea that time is money has been lost along the way.

As previously mentioned, I was not a litigator. I was a solicitor who concentrated on business-related matters, where time and money were always front and centre. If you happened to forget that idea, your client—a businessperson—would soon bring you back to the real world. Although I was not a litigator, I had occasion to attend Chambers Applications on two different days prior to my retirement. There were, I recall, thirty-five or so matters on the Chambers' list to be considered. Both days I noticed that just a small fraction of the matters were dealt with and that the balance were adjourned to a future date. I got the impression that the process was not unlike musical chairs, where the presiding Justice did everything he could to pass a matter on to the next Chambers Justice before he or she became seized with the matter. The court room was full of lawyers, all running up their hourly billings, while there seemed to be a concerted effort by the presiding Justice to avoid trying to bring various disputes to some form of resolution or at least contribute to the advancement of the litigation.

I wish to emphasize that the preceding is but my impression of what is going on within our present-day legal system. Even if I am only partly right, it should be apparent that our judicial system is just too important a pillar of our democracy to allow the present situation to continue. I believe that Justices and my former colleagues who are reading this book know in their hearts that, at the very least, there is more than just a little truth to my views on these matters.

13

GOOD CLIENTS, BETTER FRIENDS

OVER THE YEARS I have had some excellent clients who became and remain good friends and in some cases, business partners. I cannot name them all here, but two in particular I would like to acknowledge.

Brian Carlin

Brian Carlin is not a big guy, but he used his speed and finesse to play hockey in the World Hockey Association and the National Hockey League. In fact, Brian looks fit enough today to play at that level. Of course, he does not, but he plays in a competitive league with ex-professionals. He works out every day and is as strong as a horse.

I met Brian and his wife Debbie when I moved to south Calgary to open Mason & Company's south office. Brian is always fun to be around. He has a great sense of humour and when he gets to telling stories about his time playing for the Calgary Centennials with Scotty Munro and Bearcat Murray, tears roll down the cheeks of those lucky enough to hear him.

When I met Brian, he was one of four owners of a real estate company. They were located in southeast Calgary in the Lake Bonavista Shopping Centre. Their offices were very nice, and their parties were a thing of legend. South Calgary was booming, and Brian's company did very well.

As years passed, our friendship and business association grew. We both endured good times and bad but always remained friends.

Brian was extremely loyal in referring clients to me, and because of his hockey contacts, he ended up acting as a real estate agent for virtually all of the Calgary Flames of that era. He would refer these lads to me to perform the legal work associated with buying a home. It was fun meeting the guys who I watched play hockey—a game that had caught the imagination of an entire city.

Brian ended up purchasing a RE/MAX franchise, which he still owns today. He had the foresight to buy the building in which his office is located, as well as the neighbouring building.

When I announced my intent to retire from the practice of law, Brian offered me the use of one of his offices. The office was located beside Brian's office, and my job was to answer any questions related to real estate from the realtors employed by RE/MAX Landan. I would attend his company's Monday morning meetings and try to deal with problems in the real estate business that arose from time to time. My new office and job gave me a place to go in the morning, much to Brenda's delight.

Of course, Brian did not have to do this, but he did. My new office was nicer than the one I'd had at my firm. Brian and I had lots of fun visiting, going for lunch, and doing the odd business deal. Brian allowed me the opportunity to ease into retirement, a gesture I shall never forget.

Brian Carlin is a first-class individual whom I am most pleased to call my friend.

Dick Van Grieken

Dick is the absolute smartest real estate developer I have ever met in all my years of practice.

Dick came to Canada from Holland with his mother, father and sisters when he was nine years old. No one in the family spoke English when they arrived by boat in Halifax and got on a train to Alberta. Dick's family was dirt poor.

A few years ago Dick, his wife Bonnie, Brenda and I went to Halifax to explore the terminal where Dick and his family had landed. We also toured a rail car that was similar to the one the Van Grieken family had been passengers on when they headed west.

One can only imagine the stress level experienced by his parents. No money, four dependent children, no understanding of the language and no job waiting for them in Calgary. Life was tough for the family, but they did anything and everything within the law to survive. And survive they did.

Eventually Dick got involved in selling commercial real estate. While he did that, he also bought and sold houses repeatedly, eventually owning houses on one or more of the lakes located in southeast Calgary.

I am not sure of the exact date when Dick got more heavily involved in owning and developing commercial real estate. In the late 1980s or early 1990s, I started doing all his legal work, both for him personally and for his corporations.

Dick was a lawyer's dream client. He made decisions quickly, he knew what he wanted, he took advice well, and he understood commercial real estate. He was not overly demanding, but his personality and manner made you want to perform for him on a timely basis (time was really important when it came to the types of deals Dick was doing).

I am not about to breach solicitor/client privilege, but suffice it to say that Dick's business acumen has resulted in him being extremely successful.

I have had the good fortune to ride along on Dick's coattails for several lucrative ventures. The one example I would like to relate pertains to an office building we named "The Parke at Fish Creek." At the time McLeod & Company had the entire eighth floor of the Southcentre Executive Tower, but we were running out of space and were in negotiations with our landlord to take more. The landlord was being difficult, so after

yet another annoying meeting that was getting
me nowhere, I called Dick. We had, from time
to time, discussed the possibility of building an
office building together. I told Dick that it seemed
the right time to further explore the idea. Dick
came right over. We got into his vehicle and commenced touring all available, potential building
sites. Dick knew every piece of property that was
for sale in southeast Calgary. I believe the very
first site we saw was located on Bannister Road,
with frontage on Macleod Trail, a major Calgary
thoroughfare. The site was a bit awkward to get
in and out of but not bad. As I recall, the lot was
3.2 acres in size and was owned by some people
who had bid on the Toyota franchise for the area
but lost. They had no interest in keeping the land.
There had been a bit of a lull in the commercial
real estate market, but we could feel things starting to improve.

The property was purchased by Dick's company, along with a new company incorporated
by me and those of my partners who wanted to
participate in the transaction. Our new company
agreed with Dick that it would participate in purchasing forty percent of the land and the future
building. McLeod & Company would agree to rent

one third of the completed building at market rates. We had hoped to do a fifty/fifty deal with Dick, but some of my partners didn't think this was a good deal and declined to participate. However, they did not object to the firm's commitment to lease one third of the building. Dick didn't care; he was glad to pick up the extra ten percent.

Construction of the building commenced, and we built a beautiful building, one that everyone associated with the project is proud of. When I announced my retirement, Dick expressed a desire to sell the building. We sold it to a Real Estate Investment Trust (REIT), and those of us who invested in the building enjoyed a handsome profit.

Dick supervised the building and leasing of the building and did a terrific job at a very reasonable fee. When we sold the building, I had left the firm. However, notwithstanding what Dick had done for those who had invested in the building, he was required to pay his sixty-percent share of a fee charged by my old firm to do the real estate conveyancing. The fee would never, ever have been charged had I still been around. Those who invested in the building made a lot of money due to Dick's efforts and foresight, and the least my old firm could have, and should have, done was to do Dick's share of the deal for the cost of disbursements only. The fact they didn't do that ended up costing them money. Dick included me in subsequent deals but not those who were so shortsighted, unappreciative and thoughtless.

I am presently involved with Dick and others in a rather large land holding very close to one of Alberta's fastest-growing cities. I enjoy keeping in contact with Dick, and we make a point of going for lunch on a regular basis. As with Brian Carlin and Al Kolinsky, knowing Dick and spending time in his company has been a relationship that is, to say the very least, special.

14

CONCLUSION

F OR THE MOST PART, I really enjoyed the practice of law, but I especially liked the business aspect of the practice of law. I embraced the challenge of being financially successful, and I enjoyed marketing our firm and all the promotion that went with it. I worked hard and I worked long hours, all the while contributing to my community through numerous charitable or community undertakings.

Regrets...

As the song goes, "Regrets, I've had a few."

As I've mentioned, I regret not dealing with problematic partners and lawyers sooner than

I did. It shouldn't take a long period of time to determine if a lawyer is any good or not. As I previously noted, it appeared to me, I would joke, that many candidates peaked at the interview and went downhill from there. I had no problem getting rid of these folks. But others were a different story. There would be the lawyer who started out well and then did not perform. Or, I would be told by one of my partners that a certain lawyer in another area of the firm was doing a good job, only to have the numbers tell me a totally different story. For myriad reasons, partners would protect these people, and a malaise would descend upon their department. By that stage, too much time had passed, and I knew that person was not going to become a partner, at least while I was calling the shots, and I would tell the lawyer so. I wanted to be fair to the lawyer so he or she could look for a better fit with another firm. Some of these folks stayed with the firm and continued in their role as part of the pyramid's associate base.

I regret not being more generous with our staff. Although we paid them well, they did not, in hindsight, receive the monetary rewards they were due. I have asked myself why I was not more generous when, in retrospect, we could have been. My answer is this: from day one of the firm's existence, I was scared to death that we would not be successful. I wanted to guarantee the economic viability of the business. As noted, we virtually self-financed our practice, so it wasn't like partners were taking home unreasonable draws. In fact, our draws were kept to a minimum to ensure our cash flow was never at risk. In the legal business, your overhead is high and your liquidity is dependent on monthly billings maintaining a certain level. A few bad months in a row could cause financial problems. Because we were (I was) careful in managing our funds, we never got close to being in trouble. However, the risk was always present, so we were, with the benefit of hindsight, too cautious when it came to being more generous with our employees.

I have always been willing to help people when I could. As a young lawyer, I did some criminal work, but to see someone I was representing go to jail was difficult for me. I didn't handle losing civil cases well, where the law as I read it indicated I should win. If I lost a trial, for days afterwards I would wake up in the middle of the night rehashing what I could have done differently. I sometimes took my job too seriously, but I just couldn't help it.

I remember hearing about one high-profile and highly regarded lawyer who would tell his client not to forget his toothbrush at the start of a criminal trial, as his chance of acquittal wasn't good. I guess as criminal defence lawyers age and get more experience, they are less inclined to beat themselves up when their clients go to prison. The dirty truth is that most criminal clients are, in fact, guilty. However, it is the job of the defence lawyer to make the Crown prove their case beyond a reasonable doubt. If the Crown Prosecutor cannot meet that test, then for the benefit of all those charged with a crime, the accused must be acquitted. Guilty or innocent, I felt awful when I lost. I felt my job was to help a person by winning their case and preserving their freedom. People being sent to jail around Christmas time was particularly upsetting for me.

I have gone to bat for numerous people, doing them and their families huge favours. Yet memories are short, and too many people think only of themselves. Whatever you do, do not be like these folks. Guard your favours jealously, and use whatever influence you might have sparingly because, as a wise friend once noted, influence is a depreciating commodity. You will be amazed at the number of people who will quickly forget your name once you can no longer be of use to them. Do not take the slight personally; that kind of person does it to everyone.

My final tale: The Upset Builder...

One day I received a call from the general manager of a large new-home builder. He asked if he could meet with me. We arranged an appointment and met in one of our boardrooms. This fellow was, by nature, very animated; he proceeded to explain that the lawyer who had done his company's work for a considerable period of time could no longer represent his company's interests. She had discovered that she had a conflict of some sort. He was very dependent on this lawyer to convey titles to his purchasers and provide a seamless, first-class service to both his company and the home buyers and was worried that he would not be able to find another lawyer with similar abilities. He actually put his face in his hands and wondered aloud what on earth he was going to do. This fellow's company built a very large number of new homes each year. Landing such a client would be a major achievement. The man had been recommended to me by the manager of another housing division of the same corporation.

I listened sympathetically to his expressions of grief at having to find a new and no doubt inferior lawyer. All the while I was thinking: *Are you kidding me?* I knew his old lawyer; I knew how she did things and how she conducted her practice. This guy didn't know it yet, but he was in for a very big and pleasant surprise. No other law firm could provide the same level of service to builder clients that we could. No other law firm had the experienced paralegals we had, who could handle large volumes of files quickly, efficiently, properly, and well. We had at least eight very experienced and talented paralegals who could do this guy's work in their sleep. Of course, I didn't tell him that. I told him, with my tongue firmly in my cheek, that I realized we had a big job ahead of us trying to live up to the level of representation he was used to, but we would certainly try our very best.

His company files were sent to us, and they were far from being in the shape he thought they were in. A large cumulative sum of money, which had been held back pursuant to the provisions of the aforementioned Builders Lien Act, had not been released to the builder even though the lien period on many of the homes had expired long ago. His company's holdback funds had not been placed in an interest-bearing trust account, which was our practice, to give some compensation to the builder while complying with the Builders Lien Act.

We did many other things that helped the builder's cash flow. It wasn't long before this man realized what he had been missing. He sang our praises to anyone and everyone who would listen, and he and I became friends.

Remember the Golden Rules

Starting your own law firm is not an easy thing to do. It takes dedication, very hard work, more dedication and the right attitude.

You have to know how to market your legal services, and once you start getting work in the door, do it at the highest level you are capable of doing. Do not hide behind voice mail. When possible, answer your phone, and always return calls promptly. Never go home with messages unanswered. Keep your clients informed, and always put the best interests of the law firm first.

Hire the best people you can afford, and be sure to treat your trust accounts and your accounting procedures with the greatest of respect.

Advertise your services, but do it within your market area and spend your money wisely. Develop relationships with people who can send you business. Once you have a client who sends you work, never take that client for granted.

Work hard, work long, work smart. Surround yourself with hard-working, intelligent people who share your goals and desires.

Don't compromise your principles. Treat other lawyers and the Judiciary with the utmost respect even when it is difficult to do so.

And always remember my Golden Rules: Get the work in the door; do the legal work quickly, efficiently and well; promptly send out a fair account, and make sure the account is paid. If you do these four things and follow some of my suggestions to develop clientele, you are in for a rewarding career. The icing on the cake is that you will be the boss, make very good money, and not be subjected to the annoyances and the political intrigue that go hand-in-hand with working at a big firm.

Made in the USA
Columbia, SC
19 September 2018